MEN-AT-ARMS SERIE

EDITOR: MARTIN WINDR(

CH00642850

Flak Jackets

20th Century Military Body Armour

Text by SIMON DUNSTAN

Colour plates by RON VOLSTAD

OSPREY PUBLISHING LONDON

Published in 1984 by
Osprey Publishing Ltd
Member company of the George Philip Group
12–14 Long Acre, London WC2E 9LP
© Copyright 1984 Osprey Publishing Ltd

British Library Cataloguing in Publication Data

Dunstan, Simon
  Flak Jackets.—(Men-at-Arms series; 157)
  1. Arms and armor—History—20th century
  I. Title   II. Series
  623.4'41   U815
  ISBN 0-85045-569-3

Filmset in Great Britain
Printed in Hong Kong

Dedication:
To Scrat

Author's Note:
'Flak', abbreviated from 'Flugzeugabwehrkanone', the
German word for 'anti-aircraft gun', has gained common
currency as the slang term for all fragmentation
munitions, and is used in that colloquial sense in this
book. In contrast, I have used the term 'shrapnel' in
its exact sense—the pedant would argue, correctly, that
shrapnel was a specific type of ordnance discontinued
after the First World War. Finally, note that nowhere in
this book is there any reference to the 'bullet-proof vest':
there is *no such thing*.

   A list of acknowledgements will be found at the end of
the text.

Introduction

Body armour is as ancient as warfare itself. From the earliest times man has sought to protect himself from the blows and missiles of his enemies; and the materials he has used have been extraordinarily varied, dictated by local availability and craft skills as well as by the type of threat faced. The most common materials in ancient and medieval times included quilted fabrics of various kinds; bronze and iron scales and plates; flexible coats of ringmail; and many different combinations of all these materials. The working of large bronze plates reached a high degree of sophistication in ancient Greece; and the legions of early Imperial Rome were issued with ingenious flexible cuirasses of iron plates mounted on leather harness. In the High Medieval period the working of steel plate reached a peak of perfection in complete suits, proof against virtually all contemporary weapons, yet so finely articulated that the knight could move with surprising freedom.

In cultures far from Europe, armour has been devised using materials which seem to us bizarre, but which were found to be effective against local threats. In pre-conquest Mexico, quilted cotton jackets were toughened by soaking in brine, and armour was constructed from overlapped plates of hardwood. The ancient Egyptians used crocodile-skin; North American Indians used corselets of wooden rods; Gilbert Islanders used coconut fibre, to protect themselves against weapons edged with shark's teeth; and in Borneo, warriors arrayed themselves in bark armour covered with fish scales.

In the Western world the development of effective hand-held firearms led to the gradual abandonment of plate armour during the 17th century. Nevertheless, protective armour never entirely disappeared, and a range of privately purchased devices were still to be seen on the battlefields of the 19th century. The American Civil War saw the use of several popular types of armour; and one surviving breastplate, tested 100 years later, proved able to withstand a bullet from a .45cal. Colt automatic at a range of ten feet—a truly remarkable performance. Home-made armour passed into legend with the exploits of the Australian outlaw Ned Kelly, whose crude, 97lb helmet and body armour protected him from Martini Henry rifle bullets: in his 'last stand' at the Glenrowan Inn his armour stopped 17 bullets,

The first item of body armour to see widespread service in the 20th century was the military helmet. It is estimated that its use in the Great War prevented 2 to 5 per cent of the total casualties. This represents approximately 700,000 to 1,875,000 dead and wounded—a truly remarkable figure for so simple a device. Here, a wounded British soldier holds aloft his Mark I steel helmet, which was pierced by a shrapnel ball but which saved his life on the Somme battlefield, December 1916. To this day the military helmet remains the only item of body armour in many armies. (Imp. War Mus.)

although he suffered 28 wounds in the arms and legs before his capture.

On a fateful Sunday in June 1914 the Archduke Franz Ferdinand, heir to the Hapsburg thrones, failed to wear his silk protective vest—one of numerous commercially available armours advertised at the turn of the century—because of the oppressive heat of Sarajevo. The appalling aftermath of the bullet which killed him led directly to the re-introduction of military body armour by the European powers.

The Great War

At the outbreak of hostilities, none of the major combatants wore any form of protective body armour except the ceremonial cuirass and helmet of French heavy cavalry regiments, and the leather Pickelhaube worn by certain German units. The initial phase of the Great War was one of movement, but after the First Battle of Ypres this changed to positional fighting, with the entrenched armies of France and Britain facing those of Germany across a narrow strip of No Man's Land which extended from the North Sea to the Swiss frontier. Attackers and defenders were exposed to

merciless barrages of high explosive and shrapnel, while assaults were mounted frontally en masse against withering machine gun and rifle fire which produced appalling casualties.

With the advent of trench warfare the incidence of head wounds rose alarmingly, due primarily to shell fragments. Urgent measures were taken by all the warring powers to provide their soldiers with head protection; but it was the French Army that introduced the modern military helmet into actual service, thanks largely to the efforts of Sous-Intendant-Général August-Louis Adrian who, during pre-war colonial service, had been renowned for developing devices to improve the welfare of his men.

During a visit to the front line in 1914 Gen. Adrian talked to a wounded man who had been struck in the head by a shell fragment: 'I was lucky', said the sufferer casually, 'I happened to have a metal mess-bowl in my hat and it saved my life'. This incident impressed the general deeply; he promptly had a steel cap liner or 'cervelière' made and fitted inside his képi, which he wore constantly

Wearing a flexible waistcoat of scale armour, a British officer directs the retrieval of a captured German artillery piece near Mametz Wood on the Somme, 10 August 1916. Commercial vests of this type enjoyed considerable sales among frontline troops, but their protective value was marginal. They were normally worn under the uniform tunic. (Nat. Army Mus.)

to discover whether it would cause undue discomfort.

In February 1915 the Army adopted the liner, and 700,000 were ordered under the designation '*Calotte protège-tête en tôle d'acier, 1915*'. It proved difficult to convince the French 'poilu' of its effectiveness, and the 'calotte' was more often used as a cup, cooking vessel or, as a final indignity, a 'pissoir'; but despite such misuse the 'calotte' was successful, and the design of a proper military helmet proceeded rapidly. Based on the pattern worn by French 'sapeurs-pompiers' (firemen), the '*Casque modèle 1915 "Adrian", infanterie*' was adopted on 21 May. At first the 'casque Adrian' was only seen on the heads of immaculate staff officers and dignitaries visiting the battle zone. The first large-scale issue of helmets to combat units took place in time for the Champagne offensive of September 1915. By Christmas 3,125,000 had been produced, and by the end of the war almost 20 million.

The British Army quickly imitated the French and, in November 1915, manufacture began of the familiar 'tin hat' or Mark 1 steel helmet. Known also as the Brodie helmet after its inventor, the Mark 1 was originally to be made of mild steel like the 'casque Adrian'; but at the suggestion of Sir Robert Hadfield the material was changed to a steel containing 12 per cent manganese and known to this day as 'Hadfield's steel'. The wide brim of the Mark 1 was dictated by the need to give overhead protection from shell fragments and shrapnel but, unlike the French helmet, the design was well suited to mass production—by 1 July 1916 one million had been delivered. By the end of the war seven and a quarter million had been produced, including one and a half million for use by the United States Army under the designation *M1917*.

The German Army produced a steel helmet known as the 'von Gaede' at the beginning of 1915, but it was employed in only limited numbers. After considerable development work by Professors Frederick Schwerd and August Bier at the University of Hanover, the M16 Stahlhelm was adopted in November 1915. The first 30,000 were distributed among assault troops in time for the Verdun offensive of 21 February 1916. In contrast to the easily cold-formable Hadfield steel used by the British, the Germans chose a harder martensitic

Two German infantrymen wearing 'Infanterie-Panzer' stand guard with a Maxim MG08/15 machine gun on the Western Front. This is the early pattern 'Sappenpanzer' introduced in 1917. The soldier on the right has the reinforcing 'Stirnpanzer' fitted to his M16 Stahlhelm helmet. (Imp. War Mus.)

silicon/nickel steel. As a consequence, and also because of the deeper configuration, the Stahlhelm had to be hot-pressed in electrically heated dies at a far higher unit cost. It did, however, give greater protection to the head, ears and neck than either the French or British helmets but with the penalty of increased weight—2lbs 10½oz as against 1lb 11oz and 2lbs 2½oz respectively. By the end of the war, eight and a half million Stahlhelm helmets had been produced.

By late 1916 the protective helmet had been universally adopted by the armies on the Western Front—but, paradoxically, the number of soldiers with head wounds increased significantly. This was due to the fact that many of these casualties would, in the absence of the helmet, have been killed outright. Medical statistics reveal that before the introduction of the helmet one head wound in four proved fatal, but after, the ratio became as low as one in seven. Similarly, it was shown that a large percentage of wounded soldiers suffered wounds caused by missiles of low and medium velocity. Estimates vary from 60 to 80 per cent, and the proportional frequency of wounds was established as: extremities 60 per cent, head and neck 20 per cent, and torso 20 per cent.

Body Armour

While the production of the military helmet took overall priority, development was also undertaken

5

A Belgian soldier, wearing an Italian service helmet and breastplate with 'épaulières' shoulder defences, mans a forward trench on the Western Front. Most of the warring nations produced body armour during the Great War; the United States in particular developed numerous items, but few were used in combat. (Musée de l'Armée, Bruxelles)

of armour defences for other parts of the body, particularly the chest, abdomen and back since wounds in such areas were often fatal; those of the stomach had a mortality of about one in four, due generally to infection. Body armour was used in battle from 1915, but only on a limited basis. The equipment consisted for the most part of steel plates: either one-piece, shaped body shields, or multiple plates joined together in various ways, giving a range of protection levels against fragments, shrapnel and even small arms fire.

The French devised only a few items of body defence, including face shields for snipers and sentries as well as a series of visors attached to the standard helmet to protect the eyes; and an abdominal plate, also designed by Gen. Adrian. Some 100,000 of these were manufactured, but although ballistically sound they were cumbersome, and little used by the troops. Adrian also devised a breastplate which linked up with the abdominal defence. It did not see service, however, and the only body shields used in the field were commercial products such as the 'Lanciers'—see Plate B2.

In the German Army up to 500,000 heavy silicon-nickel steel breastplates were issued from May 1917 (these could in fact be worn on either the front or back). Produced in two sizes—No. 1 large and No. 2 small, weighing 24lbs and 22lbs 10oz

respectively—the 'Infanterie-Panzer' (infantry armour) was used by machine gun teams, sentinels and other troops in exposed positions. Because of its great weight it was too heavy to be worn with comfort during assaults, and its multiple-plate configuration made it too noisy for patrols; but it was favoured by the troops, who nicknamed it 'Sappenpanzer' (trench armour). It was proof against shrapnel, grenade fragments, and rifle fire at 500 yards. The Germans also issued a reinforcing plate for attachment to the ventilation lugs of the standard Stahlhelm to render the front of the helmet proof against rifle fire. Known as 'Stirnpanzer' (brow armour), it was used by snipers and sentries; 50,000 examples were made.

Of all the warring powers, the British fielded the greatest variety of body armour obtained from official and commercial agencies. Development pursued three avenues of design following the types of armour known throughout history: a rigid 'hard' armour corresponding to plate; an intermediate type of multiple small scales, corresponding to mail or brigandine work; and a yielding 'soft' armour, corresponding to the quilted defences of yore. Over a score of body shields were available from private firms, and many were purchased by men leaving for the front or by their anxious relatives. Most models seem to have given satisfaction, for all manufacturers received unsolicited letters that testified to the saving of life and limb. The Army, however, did not recommend the wholesale issue of body armour, and provided only sufficient to equip approximately two per cent of the men.

One of the earliest and most widely employed rigid models was the Dayfield Body Shield, formed of a number of separate plates protecting the chest and back. Weighing between 14 and 18lbs depending on configuration, over 20,000 sets were in use on the Western Front by October 1917; but again, it was often discarded as a hindrance by the fighting troops. For this reason continuous efforts were made to lighten the various armours, which had the effect of reducing ballistic efficiency. Here once more was the armourer's age-old problem: heavy but effective models were unpopular, but lighter variants were despised for their lack of protection.

Numerous variants of rigid body shields were produced, weighing generally between 5 and 10lbs and providing ballistic protection on a par with that of the Mark 1 steel helmet. Of these some notable examples were the 'Best Body Shield', the 'Portobank' armoured waistcoat, the government issue 'BEF' (British Expeditionary Forces) model, the 'Star' body defence and the 'Army and Navy' body shield. In an effort to provide a standard issue armour the Munitions Inventions Board finally manufactured the 'EOB' (Experimental Ordnance Board) model in 1917. It weighed $9\frac{1}{2}$lbs and was formed of three elements: a breastplate, backplate and groin protector. It gave protection against shrapnel and grenade fragments, and it could resist a .45cal. pistol bullet at 800 feet/second or a rifle ball at 1,000 feet/second. In the last two years of the war the 'EOB' was issued in fairly substantial numbers.

Of the intermediate type of armour, the majority of models were formed of small square plates of metal attached to a canvas support covering the chest and back in the form of a scaled waistcoat, or 'brigandine'. Garments such as 'Berkeley's Flexible Armour Guard', the 'Franco-British Cuirass' and 'Wilkinson's Safety Service Jacket' enjoyed considerable sales because of their low weight of about 3lbs. Being closely fitting, they were considered comfortable, but they gave little protection except against very low-velocity projectiles such as expended shrapnel balls or small shell splinters. If struck by a bullet, one of the scales was apt to be pushed into the wearer's body causing horrendous wounds or death.

In the field of 'soft' body armour, the Munitions Inventions Board conducted numerous experiments with fibrous materials such as balata, kapok, flax, hair, cotton, sisal, hemp and silk. Whereas steel plate defeated projectiles by its rigidity and hardness at the point of impact, the aim of soft armour was to slow and trap the projectile so that

Men of the New Zealand Medical Corps dispense tea to German prisoners during the Third Battle of Ypres, 5 October 1917. The men at extreme left and right are wearing Dayfield Body Shields. (Imp. War Mus.)

Typical of the many commercial models of body armour available during the Great War is the Pullman A.1. Shield. It featured in an advertisement in 'The War Dragon', the Buffs' regimental magazine, of October 1916. (W. Y. Carman Collection)

penetration was arrested by the strength of the garment as a whole. It was concluded that silk was the most resistant fibre and was superior to manganese steel, weight for weight, against shrapnel balls up to a velocity of 900–1,000 feet/second. It did not give nearly the same protection against high-velocity pointed projectiles such as rifle bullets or bayonet thrusts, but neither did it deform a bullet when perforated. A bullet which pierces steel plate is invariably deformed, and often causes more serious wounds than one which passes through the body cleanly. Thus it was evident that against low-velocity blunt projectiles up to a certain velocity, such as shrapnel, shell splinters and grenade fragments (the causes of the majority of wounds) silk was an effective body defence and superior to steel at the same weight.

The first application of silk as armour was a 'necklet' covering the shoulders and neck with a high Queen Anne 'Ulster' collar, nearly 2in. thick and weighing $3\frac{1}{4}$lbs. In 1915 it was issued at a scale of 400 to a division, but proved less satisfactory

than had been supposed. On the sodden battlefields of Flanders silk deteriorated rapidly; it was expensive, and more difficult to procure than steel. Alternative materials were sought, culminating in the 'Chemico Body Shield' (see Plate A1) manufactured by the County Chemical Company of Birmingham for the British Army. This heavily padded waistcoat weighed about 6lbs and was composed of multiple layers of tissue, linen scraps, cotton and silk, bonded together by a resinous substance. It was cheap, comfortable to wear, and capable of resisting a .45cal. pistol bullet at 300 feet/second. Of all the body defences devised during the Great War, the 'Chemico' was in many ways the most interesting. It featured materials and technology known to the Assyrians 3,000 years ago; yet in application and configuration it was remarkably similar to most of today's body armours.

To sum up, body armour was not extensively used during the Great War except in particular circumstances where it often proved to be effective. Although, throughout the war, fragmentation weapons caused the greatest number of casualties, it was the machine gun that was most feared. This weapon had aborted all the earlier offensives, causing approximately 35 per cent of casualties, and soldiers needed a defence against it. Body armour that only resisted low- and medium-velocity projectiles could scarcely satisfy them; and body armour capable of thwarting a rifle bullet was too heavy and cumbersome in the assault.

The Second World War

During the inter-war period experimentation in body armour was minimal. In the United States research into helmet design continued at a leisurely pace until the resurgence of military expenditure in 1940. On 30 April 1941 the M1 helmet—a two-piece design with an outer Hadfield steel shell and a separate inner liner containing the suspension system—was standardised, and it was approved on 9 June 1941. Between August 1941 and August 1945, 22,363,015 M1 helmets were produced—the single most common item of armour ever made.

In Europe the nations' soldiers went into action with helmets very similar to those of the Great War.

No other form of armour was worn; but in October 1940 the British Army Council instructed the Medical Research Council (MRC) to investigate the feasibility of an 'armour-plated suit' within a weight limit of 4lbs for combat troops, and a heavier one of up to 10lbs for use by predominantly static troops such as anti-aircraft or naval gun crews. After resurrecting the dusty files of Great War casualty statistics, and examining the types of wounds sustained by Dunkirk survivors to discover which areas of the body most required protection, the Body Protection Committee of the MRC produced a set of body armour in February 1941.

The MRC Body Armour consisted of three separate 1mm-thick manganese steel plates with a total weight of $2\frac{3}{4}$lbs. The chest plate, measuring 9ins. × 8ins., was to protect the heart, great blood vessels and lung roots; the 14 by 4in. back plate was worn below the shoulder blades to protect the base of the lungs, the liver and, by means of a 5in. upward projection, a portion of the spine; while the third plate, measuring 8 by 6ins., was worn over the abdomen. The plates were attached to each other by webbing straps and were slightly curved to conform to the contours of the body. The complete set with canvas covers and webbing weighed $3\frac{1}{2}$lbs.

Five thousand sets were manufactured for evaluation trials with units of the Home Forces and troops in the Middle East. First impressions of the body armour were highly favourable; in tests it withstood a .38cal. pistol bullet at five yards, a .303

Men of the British 56th Inf. Div. don the MRC Body Armour during a training exercise in the 11th Corps area of Eastern Command, 21 March 1942. The photograph shows the correct method of wear under the battledress. (Imp. War Mus.)

bullet at 700 yards, and a 'Tommy Gun' single shot at 100 yards. In April 1942 approval was given for the introduction of the 'MRC Body Armour' into the British Army. After further field exercises it was found that the armour, although well padded, tended to cut into the soft-skin areas of the body causing chafing, with the result that violent and rapid movements were significantly impaired. Moreover, it caused a man to perspire so profusely that his powers of endurance were affected.

From late 1942 enthusiasm for the equipment began to wane, and when it was realised that the production of body armour would compete for the scant resources required for the manufacture of steel helmets, priority was given to the latter. It was not until September 1943 that the War Office placed an order with the Ministry of Supply for 500,000 suits—subsequently reduced to 300,000. Within a few months the order was completed by large steel firms in the north of England, with production ceasing at 200,000 sets. Of these, 79,000 were issued to the Forces: 15,000 to the Army and 64,000 to the Royal Air Force. The remaining 121,000 were kept in War Office stores. Some 12,000 sets were sent to 21 Army Group, where the major portion was allocated to the Airborne Divisions, with smaller quantities to the Canadian Army, SAS troops and the Polish Parachute Brigade; some 300 sets were also sent to Italy for use by Royal Engineers engaged in special duties. The MRC Body Armour was rarely used in action; the only confirmed occasion was by the Airborne Forces during Operation 'Market Garden' (see Plate B2).

Two other forms of British body armour were designed during the Second World War: the 'Armorette' and the 'Wisbrod Armoured Vest'. The Armorette was composed of metal plates embedded in a vulcanised rubber foundation which gave a high degree of flexibility. The Wisbrod vest utilised cloth-covered steel plates which overlapped to provide protection to the front of the thorax and the abdomen. Neither proceeded beyond the development stage. Both these models and the MRC Body Armour were evaluated in the United States by the Army Ordnance Department. It was concluded that any advantages of such armour would be very slight when set against the overall loss of combat efficiency and the increase in the soldier's load. In November 1942 it was decided that individual body armour for ground troops seemed to be a military luxury that could be ill afforded during a global conflict, and overall interest declined. Nevertheless, in April 1943 the Army Ordnance Department submitted an endorsement to the Army Air Forces stating that it had rejected the concept of body armour because of the perceived loss of mobility to ground troops, but that an application might well be found for Air Force combat personnel.

Aircrew armours

The initial impetus to the development of body armour for the combat crewmen of the US Army Air Forces was due to the research and field trials of the British MRC Body Armour. In early October 1942 an analysis of wounds incurred by US 8th Air Force combat personnel revealed that approximately 70 per cent were due to missiles of relatively low velocity—in one survey involving 303 casualties it was found that 38 per cent of wounds were due to 'flak' fragments; 39 per cent to 20mm cannon shell fragments; 15 per cent to machine gun bullets; and 8 per cent to secondary missiles

USAAF bomber crewmen display the early experimental flyer's body armour—on the left, the Type B half-vest and Type C tapered apron for pilots and co-pilots, and on the right, the Type A full vest and Type D full apron for gunners, navigators, bombardiers and radio operators. (USAF)

(primarily parts of the aircraft breaking up when hit by flak or cannon fire). Col. (later Brig. Gen.) Malcolm C. Grow, then surgeon of the 8th Air Force, had followed the British trials with interest and realised that some form of armour protecting the chest and abdomen could reduce both mortality (deaths) and morbidity (the total number of wounds) among combat aircrews.

Grow chose manganese steel as the ballistic material, and, in association with the Wilkinson Sword Company Ltd of London, formulated plans for a vest made of overlapping 2in.-square plates of 1mm-thick Hadfield steel secured in pockets in a canvas cover backed by a cotton fleece material. On 15 October 1942 Lt. Gen. Carl A. Spaatz, Commanding General, 8th Air Force, approved an order for ten protective vests for experimental testing; this order was increased shortly afterward to a number sufficient to equip the crews of 12 B-17 bombers. These suits were fabricated by Wilkinsons, who had been making body armour on a commercial basis since the Great War; they were delivered in March 1943.

The experimental flyer's armour proved highly successful; and Lt. Gen. Ira C. Eaker, who had assumed command of the 8th Air Force, directed that enough body armour—commonly known as 'flak suits'—should be produced in England to equip 60 per cent of all bomber crews located there (this being the normal percentage of aircraft available for operations on any given day). While manufacture was begun in England (a total of 600 suits were made), samples were despatched in July 1943 to the United States, where they were produced in quantity on a priority basis. By the end of the war approximately 23 types of flyer's body armour were in production, and almost one million items had been manufactured.

The initial production of the armour in the United States was based solely on the design which had been developed by Col. Grow. Classified as Flyer's Vest, M1, it was made up of two sections which provided front and back protection, and was closed at the shoulders by quick-release 'do' fasteners. It was issued to gunners, navigators, bombardiers and radio operators, whose combat duties required them to move around the aircraft where they were exposed to injury from both front and back. It weighed 17lbs 6oz. Between August

943 and August 1945, 338,780 M1 vests were produced. Their effectiveness can be gauged by this account from 2nd Lt. Harold E. Donley, a bombardier of 553rd Squadron, 386th Bombardment Group:

'While participating on a mission over enemy territory, 3 November 1943, I was struck above the heart by a piece of flak two inches long by one-half inch square. The blow knocked me flat on my back from a kneeling position. The flak suit suffered very little damage but did a good job of stopping the piece of jagged steel. I think the protection offered by the suit greatly outweighs the discomfort it causes the wearer. In my estimation it is one of the most valuable pieces of protective equipment issued to combat crews.'

The *Flyer's Vest, M2*, was very similar to the M1 but had only an armoured front, since it was used by pilots and co-pilots who sat in armoured seats providing back protection. It weighed 7lbs 15oz;

A mine-clearing party equipped with protective clothing and improvised skis probe for Schumines during the closing weeks of the Second World War. The skis are intended to take the initial shock of an explosion, and the light-steel alloy leg guards and padded clothing to deflect the blast. Note the cut-down respirator protecting the eyes of the leading man. (*Soldier magazine*)

and between August 1943 and July 1945 95,919 vests were produced. Both the M1 and M2 vests were standardised on 5 October 1943. They differed slightly from the English model in that the original linen canvas was unavailable in the United States and a cotton canvas was substituted, later superseded by ballistic nylon.

In addition to the vest, an apron section was suspended from it to provide protection for the abdomen, groin and upper thighs. A number of models were produced to be worn by various crew members, depending upon their position and function in the aircraft. The *Flyer's Apron, M3*, was a triangular piece of armour intended for use in turrets and other confined positions. It weighed 4lbs 14oz, and 142,814 were produced. The *Flyer's Apron, M4*, was similar to the M3 but square in configuration, for use by waist gunners and others who benefited from a greater area of protection—see Plate B1. It weighed 7lbs 2oz, and 209,144 were produced. S/Sgt. Earl E. Koehler, a waist gunner of 401st Bombardment Group, recalls:

'On 11 January 1944, after we had made our bomb run, we were in the midst of a mass German attack. A 20mm cannon shell entered the radio room, hit the left side of my flak suit and exploded. I was knocked down and dazed until my oxygen was again hooked to a walk-around bottle. After we landed I was taken to the field dispensary and was found to have a bruised side. In my opinion the flak suit had saved another life.'

For seated personnel, the *Groin Armor, M5* was provided, comprising three sections so that the central area could be drawn between the legs and the side sections spread over the upper thighs—see Plate B3. The entire piece could be attached to the M2 vest. It weighed 15lbs 4oz, and 109,901 were produced.

All these items were worn over other flying equipment, including parachutes, so provision for the rapid jettisoning of the armour in an emergency was essential—a safe parachute landing could be jeopardised by the additional weight of armour. The various combinations of vest and apron were attached to one another by quick release dot fasteners which were connected by tapes, so that a single pull on a red tab at the wearer's waist caused the various items of armour to fall away instantly,

Twins serving with 1st Marine Tank Bn. in Korea display the first-pattern Vest, Armored, M-1951, with its exposed zipper and equipment loop around the midriff. The Doron plates are readily discernible under the outer covering. (USMC)

leaving the aircrewman free to jump without impediment.

By the beginning of 1944 approximately 13,500 flak suits were in use with the 8th and 9th Air Forces. They were issued individually to crews going on missions, and surrendered on their return, so that all bomber groups had sufficient to enable every despatched man to wear one. Early in 1944 flyer's armour was introduced into the 12th Air Force, and into the 15th Air Force soon afterwards, so that by May a headquarters memorandum stated that 'reasonably full use is being made of body armor by crews in the theater' (Italy).

Continued research into lighter ballistic materials to reduce the weight of the armour resulted in the *Flyer's Vest, M6* and *M7*. They fulfilled the same function as the M1 and M2 vests which they superseded, but incorporated aluminium plates and ballistic nylon stock. Apron armour was similarly improved, and the *Flyer's Apron, M8* and *M9*, were standardised in July 1945 for use with the M6 and M7 vests. In the Pacific theatre, where backpack parachutes were favoured over the seat parachutes used in Europe, the vests were modified to fit over them, giving rise to the *M6A1* and *M7A1* models. Flyer's armour was not as extensively used in the Pacific, since the flak and fighter threat was considerably less than that encountered in Europe.

At the outset bomber crews were issued with the standard M1 helmet as head protection, but it was rarely worn since it interfered with flying goggles,

headphones and oxygen masks. In consequenc aircrews suffered a disproportionately high in cidence of head wounds, which caused over a thir of combat fatalities. After the introduction of th 'Grow helmet' or M4, these were substantiall reduced. The *Helmet, M4* was of the skullcap typ composed of overlapping Hadfield steel plates in cover of fabric and leather—see Plate B1—wit openings at the sides to permit the wearing c headphones. The *M4A1* was similar but feature armoured earplates to cover the headphones. Th *M4A2* was a later model which was made slightl longer to accommodate all head sizes. The M helmet was primarily for turret and tail gunner whose 'working space' was at a premium. For thos crew members with no such limitations a modifie M1 helmet was provided which featured hinge earplates over the cutaway headphone area. Th *Helmet, M3* was standardised in December 194 and 213,543 were produced. In January 1945 a improved model of reduced dimensions but greate armour protection was standardised as the *Helme M5*—see Plate B3.

To provide protection to the vulnerable nec area where it was exposed between the helmet an armoured vest, the *Armor, Neck, T44* was introduce experimentally in 1945, and 10,969 were produce before development terminated in June. It was we received, but the war ended before standardisatio a later model, T59E2, was standardised as *Arm Neck, M13* in September 1945. From October 194 to July 1944 numerous designs of face armour we studied concurrently with the development flyer's helmets. Both metallic and non-metall materials were tested in models that covered th lower part of the face, the neck and the oxyge mask. The project was suspended in 1944 becau no specific requirement for this type of armou existed.

As to the effectiveness of flyer's body armou numerous casualty surveys among heavy bomb crews were conducted at various times. They concluded that flak suits were highly successful decreasing the total number of wounds and th number of lethal wounds in the protected area Prior to the adoption of body armour the casual rate was 5.44 men wounded and 6.53 wounds p 1,000 aircrewmen despatched on missions. In th period November 1943 to May 1944, after th

ntroduction of body armour, 684,350 aircrewmen
vent on missions and 1,567 men became casualties
vith a total of 1,766 wounds: this gave a casualty
ate of 2.29 wounded and 2.58 wounds per 1,000.
Thus, after the adoption of body armour there was a
eduction of 58 per cent in persons wounded and a
eduction of 60 per cent in the total number of
ounds sustained.

Body armour also reduced fatalities significantly.
There was a reduction in deaths from thoracic
chest) wounds from 36 to 8 per cent, and from
bdominal wounds from 39 to 7 per cent. Overall,
ody armour prevented approximately 74 per cent
f wounds in the body regions covered; a fact that
nd Lt. Thomas D. Sellers, a co-pilot of 535th
quadron, 381st Bombardment Group, learnt in
ie hardest school of all—in the skies over Germany
uring a mission on 8 October 1943:

   'On previous raids I had found that the flak
   suit and helmet were major mental comforts,
   but on this flight 20mm cannon shells exploded
   inside the cockpit and knocked me down in my
   seat. The fragmentation ripped up everything.
   Wiring was torn loose, top glasses and windows
   were shattered, and the hydraulic system was
   shot out.

   'My whole side not covered by the flak suit
   was splotched with wounds but even though
   my suit was torn and dented, nowhere on the
   trunk of my body was I even scratched. . . To
   those who may object to the weight I can say
   truthfully that you'll never notice it in the heat
   of battle. It gets lighter with each mile you go
   inside enemy territory until finally you wonder
   if it is heavy enough to do the job. . . All in all, it
   has more than done its job for me.'

                *   *   *

Following the widespread use and acceptance of
er's armour, other branches of the fighting forces
came interested in its possibilities. In October
43 Motor Torpedo Boat Squadron Number 25
perimented with flyer's armour. Similarly the
avalry Board at Fort Riley, Kansas, was also
terested in its possible use by mechanised cavalry
rsonnel. In mid-1944 interest in body armour for
ound troops was rekindled at the Army Ordnance
epartment, due largely to the success of flyer's
mour and to the work of Lt.Col. I. Ridgeway

Members of the 27th Inf. Regt., US 25th Inf. Div., model the
Armor, Vest, M12 (left) and the Armor, Vest, Nylon, T-52-1
(right). Note the increased body coverage of the latter,
particularly of the thorax. (US Army)

Trimble, then chief of the surgical service at the
118th General Hospital in Sydney, Australia. After
a great deal of difficulty, he was able to obtain in
February 1943 an example of body armour used by
Japanese troops. There were at least three types of
Japanese body armour in service, comprising an
anterior thoraco-abdominal shield with or without
lower limb protection. After further investigation he
refined the design, and fabricated a model for
possible use by the Allies. An experimental body
armour known as *Vest, T34* was based on Trimble's
work. It consisted of overlapping 0.684in.-thick
carbon steel plates in a stitched nylon-web backing.
Owing to its excessive weight and the emergence of
lighter ballistic materials, the T34 series was
discontinued.

   Thereafter, numerous other experimental models
were developed. Of these, the *Vest, T62E1* proved
most promising and, after further modification in
the T64 series, it was standardised in August 1945 as
the *Armor, Vest, M12*. During the previous month
1,000 T62E1 vests (with T65 apron) and 1,200 T64
vests were shipped to the Pacific theatre for field
testing, but this was never accomplished. The M12
vest consisted of two sections, front and back, which
were fastened together at the shoulders by quick-

release fasteners in the same manner as flyer's armour. The ballistic materials consisted of 0.125in.-thick 75 ST aluminium plates and a backing of 8-ply nylon cloth. It weighed 12lbs 3oz, and 53,352 vests were produced between June and September 1945.

The M12 marked the culmination of the use of metal as the ballistic material for body armour. More importantly, it represented the final acceptance by the ground forces of the desirability of body armour as a standard item of equipment. Unfortunately this lesson was learned too late in the Second World War to benefit the infantryman, who stood most in need of protection. Statistics from 57 US divisions in the European theatre of operations indicate that foot soldiers, comprising 68.5 per cent of the total Army strength, suffered 94.5 per cent of its casualties. It was further established that shell or mortar fragments caused from 60 to 80 per cent of the wounds—figures almost identical to those of the Great War.

The Korean War

In early 1943 the US Naval Research Laborator became interested in the possibility of fabricating lightweight body armour for use by Marine groun troops and exposed shipboard personnel. At th same time the Military Planning Division, Office the Quartermaster General, was investigating th feasibility of non-metallic ballistic materials fo body armour and helmets, both to reduce th overall weight of the items and because of th critical shortage of metals. In May 1943 the Do Chemical Company succeeded in developing promising material consisting of layers of gla

The crew of an M43 8in. GMC pose by their vehicle, which sheltered in an 'elephant hide' near the 'Punchbowl', 3 Ju 1953. All the crew members are wearing M12 vests; t corporal on the left has his vest back to front. With t adoption of the M-1952 vest the earlier M12 models we issued to support troops, such as artillerymen, and to oth contingents of the United Nations forces in Korea. (US Arm

laments bonded together with an ethyl cellulose resin under high pressure. The glassfibre laminate was named 'Doron' after Col. (later Brig. Gen.) Georges F. Doriot, then director of the Military Planning Division.

Because of the bi-service interest in the possibities of Doron, a Joint Army-Navy Plastic Armor Technical Committee was established, headed by Col. Doriot and Rear Admiral Alexander H. Van Keuren. Further research demonstrated that ethyl cellulose did not give adequate ballistic performance at extreme temperatures. Accordingly, a new resin to bond the glass cloth was developed (methacrylate) which gave superior performance over a wider temperature range. This improved material was referred to as Doron Type 2. Ballistic research indicated that a $\frac{1}{16}$in. plate of 8-ply Doron Type 2 was just sufficient to stop a .45cal., 230-grain bullet fired from the standard service automatic pistol at a velocity of 800 feet/second. On the basis of these tests it was decided to use $\frac{1}{8}$in., 15-ply Doron Type 2 for service use. This thickness ensured a safety factor of two over that required to defeat a .45cal. bullet, and this number of plies gave maximum body coverage compatible with comfort and mobility.

At this stage the Army Ordnance Department decided that, as a ballistic material for body armour, nylon-aluminium combinations were superior to Doron, and its development programme culminated in the production of the *Armor, Vest, T2*. The Navy continued to favour Doron, however, which seemed highly suitable for shipboard personnel and amphibious troops, not only because of its ballistic properties in resisting shell fragments but also because of its low weight in water compared to metallic armour.

During further studies into the mechanics of body armour conducted under the auspices of the Bureau of Medicine and Surgery by Lt.Cdrs. Andrew P. Webster, USNR, and Edward L. Corey, USNR, several important factors emerged. The detrusion factor was particularly significant. Detrusion or 'dishing' refers to the depth and area to which the armour is deformed under missile impact. If the 'dish' or identation is deep, severe injury or even death may result, even though the projectile does not penetrate the armour. This factor is now called 'blunt impact trauma' and is a fundamental

A Marine holds the M-1951 armoured vest that saved his life when a Chinese 'burp gun' (PPSh41) was fired at him from a distance of 20 feet. His only injury is the heavy bruise on his right side, which illustrates the effect of 'blunt trauma'. (USMC)

consideration in the design of any 'soft' body armour. Also, the importance of incorporating large plates in the body armour became clear. By the law of the conservation of momentum, the object which a missile strikes will acquire a velocity inversely proportional to its mass. Experiments showed that small 2in.-square plates tended to be driven into the body, whereas large plates, because of their greater mass, resisted a projectile with reduced acquired velocity, and also had less tendency to deflect, which might allow a missile to ricochet past.

In order to ascertain whether an inner padding was necessary between the armour and the body to alleviate detrusion, experiments were performed by firing a .45cal. automatic pistol from 15 feet using the human hand as the test object. Lt.Cdr. Alexander Webster recounts:

A Marine rifleman in Korea adopts a firing position on the battleline wearing an M-1951 vest and 'lower torso armor', which was designed to protect the abdomen and those 'assets' so precious to all soldiers. It was nicknamed the 'diaper' by Marines, and was used in limited numbers in both the Korean and Vietnam Wars. (USMC)

'Dr Corey, with a great deal of physical courage, volunteered to be the subject of this test. The strain of this first test is understood when one considers that we did not know whether his arm would be torn off by the blow from the bullet or whether I would even hit the armor on his hand. The shots proceeded as follows. When Doron was backed with 1in. sponge rubber or a heavy layer of kapok, the impact of the bullet on the hand resulted in no discomfort, and even with a few thicknesses of duck cloth no injury resulted. The bullets were literally picked out of the air and caught as if catching marbles flipped at the hand. When the backing was reduced to a single thickness of duck cloth, severe bruising resulted, with hematoma, pain and edema, but without fracture. Deep sensation did not return in the hand for a period of about six weeks. It was concluded from these experiments that since our problem of armouring ground troops and shipboard personnel was one involving maximum protection and comfort for minimum weight, no backing should be used.'

By now a sufficiently detailed concept of the requirements of a practical body armour had been achieved to address the problems of fundamental design of a garment which would be light in weight, comfortable, and capable of being worn aboard ship or with the equipment of combat troops. The final design involved the simple expedient of

placing the Doron plates in sheathlike pockets sewn to the inside of the standard issue Marine Corps utility jacket and to the outside of the standard Navy kapok life jacket. Both types were demonstrated before representatives of various agencies. During the demonstrations Lt.Cdr. Corey wore both jackets, and was shot in the side with a .45cal. automatic pistol fired by Lt.Cdr. Webster. The demonstration was repeated 21 times with no serious injury. As a result, the Marine Corps ordered 1,000 jackets to equip a full battalion of landing troops, and they were issued to 2nd Marine Division of III Amphibious Corps in time for the Okinawa invasion of April 1945. As it happened the division remained in reserve and only a few of the armoured utility jackets were used in the final phase of fighting.

Experiments were resumed after the Second World War at the Naval Medical Field Research Laboratory at Camp Lejeune, North Carolina, where a simple, slipover type of vest incorporating curved Doron plates was in the process of development under the direction of Lt.Cdr Frederick C. Lewis, (MSC), USN. At the same time the Biophysics Division of the Chemical Corps

Soldiers of 443rd QM Group model three types of flak jacket used in Korea: (left) the Flyer's, Vest, M6; (right) the second pattern Marine M-1951 with right-over-left snap-fastener flap covering the zipper; and (centre) the US Army nylon T-52-3 vest which was standardised in October 1952 as Armor, Vest, M-1952. It features a fly front, dash-type pockets with grenade loops above, and bandolier retaining straps at the shoulder. (US Army)

Medical Laboratories was undertaking basic research in the fields of wound ballistics and body armour, using materials including nylon, Doron, steel and aluminium in various combinations to ascertain the relative protection they afforded animal tissue against various types of missiles.

With the outbreak of war in Korea in June 1950 the Biophysics Division despatched a wound ballistics team to the Far East Command. On its return to the United States, the team reported in May 1951. Among its findings were that approximately 92 per cent of wounds were caused by fragments, primarily mortar and grenade, as opposed to approximately 7.5 per cent by small arms; 72.7 per cent of wounds were of a penetrating, as opposed to 20.3 per cent of a perforating type. Having also noted the protective effects of ordinary items of clothing—finding, for example, that bullets remained in the foot even when shot through the boot at very close range, as in self-inflicted wounds—the team concluded that some form of body armour was both feasible and desirable.

Meanwhile, 500 of the Doron-armoured utility jackets as used at Okinawa were airlifted to the 1st Marine Division during the Inchon-Seoul operation of September 1950. Most of them went astray during the sealift to Wonsan, and only 50 garments were issued to the Division Reconnaissance Company at the time of the epic Chosin Reservoir battles. Understandably, this unit kept no records, but the commanding officer, Maj. Walter Gall, USMC, credited the armoured jackets with saving several lives.

Acting on the recommendations of the wound ballistics team, the Army conducted further laboratory tests into suitable ballistic materials for an armoured vest. Steel was rejected because of its lack of flexibility and excessive weight. Aluminium proved to have a relatively low ballistic limit, and was difficult to tailor into a garment with adequate flexibility. Despite its proven performance against shell fragments, the Army once again rejected Doron because it also lacked the desired flexibility, and because fibreglass splinters have unpleasant properties if introduced into a wound. Nylon cloth (12 layers of 2 × 2 basket weave) was found to give the required ballistic protection against simulated fragments, and its great flexibility was well suited for fabrication into an armoured vest.

Armed with these findings, the Army conferred with the Naval Field Medical Research Laboratory at Camp Lejeune, where models of the Doron slipover vest were held. It was agreed to incorporate into the vest certain modifications including the addition of 12 layers of nylon to the area covering the shoulder girdle. The modified vest was described as: 'A slip-over, semi-flexible thoraco-abdominal vest weighing 6.1lbs made of 2 × 2 basket-weave nylon covering the upper chest and shoulder girdle, and a lower portion made of 16 curved Doron plates covering the lower chest and upper abdomen. Ballistic properties as follows:

A classic image of the 'grunt' in Vietnam, as a Marine with an M-1955 armoured vest gives himself an impromptu shower with his M-1 helmet. In March 1961 an improved liner of ballistic nylon was introduced for the M1 which raised its protective level by some 15 per cent. The M1 helmet is credited with reducing casualties by 8 per cent during the Vietnam War. (Tim Page)

capable of stopping a .45cal. pistol or Thompson sub-machine gun bullet at the muzzle; all the fragments of the USA hand grenade at three feet; 7. per cent of the USA 81mm mortar at ten feet; and the full thrust of an American bayonet.'

In June 1951, 50 of these vests were fabricated at Camp Lejeune. On 14 June a joint Army-Navy medical mission was despatched to the Far East Command for the purpose of field testing the body armour under combat conditions. The team arrived at the headquarters of 5th Regiment, 1st Marine Division in Korea on Independence Day. Only 40 vests were available, and these were rotated among as many wearers as possible in the three regiments selected for the trial—the 5th Marines and the 23rd and 38th Infantry Regiments of the US 2nd Infantry Division. During the course of the following two months the vests were worn by approximately 6,000 Marines and soldiers in the Inje and 'Punchbowl' areas. The troops were carefully indoctrinated in the use and in the protective ballistic properties of the nylon body armour—nylon being more associated in their minds with alluring feminine attire than with protection from shell fragments.

Once this psychological hurdle was overcome, troop acceptance was almost unanimous, particularly among fire-fight veterans. It was proved that body armour could be worn for operations in rugged, mountainous terrain in a hot, humid climate with only a few complaints about additional weight. The principal criticism of the vest was that it became excessively hot, and that a water-resistant fabric cover was needed to prevent gain in weight from perspiration or rain. This could be as much as 1½ to 2lbs—a significant increase over the initial 6.1lb weight of the armour.

The Marine initiative

Upon its return to the United States in September 1951, the joint Army-Navy mission recommended that approximately 1,400 vests incorporating changes suggested by the Korean field trial be made, to be followed by additional combat tests. The Marine Corps realised that speed was of the essence, however, and on 16 November the Commandant approved the standardisation and procurement of 500 vests for airlift to 1st Marine Division in Korea by not later than 31 January

952. With only weeks remaining before the deadline, the vest was redesigned time and again until the armour came within a weight limit of 8lbs without any sacrifice in protection. A plastic fibre manufacturer agreed to supply 70,000 Doron plates, and a Philadelphia sportswear company contracted for the first 500 vests, plus an additional ,500 to be delivered by 30 March 1951. The armour was immediately put into production as the *Vest, Armored, M-1951*.

The M-1951, weighing 7¾lbs, was described as: 'A zippered, vest-type sleeveless jacket constructed of water-resistant nylon incorporating two types of armor. One, a flexible pad of basket-weave nylon, covers the upper chest and shoulder girdle; the other, overlapping curved Doron plates, covers the lower chest, back and abdomen... Although the ballistic properties of the flexible pads of basket-weave nylon and the Doron plates are virtually the same, by using the rigid plates where flexibility is not mandatory the problem of protrusion [blunt impact trauma] and the resultant wounds under the armor is reduced.'

The first 500 vests reached Korea within days of the deadline, and were issued to the 1st and 7th Marines for field trials. In his first letter to Headquarters, Marine Corps, dated 4 February

Two crew members of an M48A3 of 1/77th Armor sit atop their tank wearing M69 flak jackets. The principal external differences of the M69 as compared to the M-1952 are the 3/4-collar and the deletion of the shoulder straps. Against standing orders flak jackets were frequently worn open in Vietnam because of the heat, thus providing no protection to the vulnerable thoraco-abdominal region. (Tim Page)

1952, the project officer, Capt. David R. McGrew, Jr., USMC, wrote '. . . up to tonight we have had nine men hit while wearing the vest. One was killed outright as a 120mm mortar round landed right in his lap. However, the other eight showed excellent results. All of the eight were wounded in other places not covered by the vest—but they are all WIA instead of KIA.' He cited the case of a rifleman of 2nd Bn., 7th Marines who was wounded by the explosion of an 82mm mortar round only 15 feet in front of him. He received several fragments in the face and his leg was fractured, but there were 45 holes in his vest without any penetration. Fifteen of the fragments had been large enough to inflict mortal chest or abdomen wounds.

Early results proved conclusively that the M-1951 armoured vest reduced battle casualties by as much as 30 per cent, with the largest reduction in the KIA category. Most authoritative Marine statistics indicate that body armour prevented 60 to 70 per cent of chest and abdominal wounds, and

South Koreans of the ROK 2nd Marine 'Blue Dragon' Brigade retrieve their dead after a battle near Gia Quang, March 1967, in which a Viet Cong battalion was annihilated: its forward scouts were silently despatched by '*tae-kwan-do*', a fearsome Korean martial art, then the main body was drawn into a devastating killing zone. These ROKs are wearing M-1952 flak jackets and M1 helmets. (Tim Page)

that from 25 to 30 per cent of wounds occurring through the vest were reduced in severity. Further, as one Marine report concluded: 'There are no records to indicate what in all probability is the most significant figure—the number of cases where the wearer was hit but did not become a casualty at all.' An additional 2,500 vests arrived in Korea early in March 1952, and on 13 March 1st Marine Division ordered 25,000 more. By 14 July 1952 9,772 armours, sufficient to equip all frontline troops on a rotation basis, were on hand in the division—the armoured vest had become a standard item of Marine equipment.

In the meantime, the Army had developed an all-nylon vest covered with a vinyl-coated nylon poncho material, olive drab in colour, with a $\frac{1}{4}$in. layer of sponge rubber beneath the covering over the ribs and the shoulder girdle. The sponge rubber served to offset the vest from the body to alleviate contusions or fractures which might have resulted from the impact of non-penetrating missiles. On 18 February the Body Armor Test Team left for Korea with the aim of testing the experimental nylon body armour in combat under the codename Operation 'Boar'. At the outset there were only 48 vests available; they were classified *Armor, Vest, Nylon, T-52-1*. During the course of the test, from 1 March 1952 to 15 July 1952, a total of 1,400 T-52-1 vests were worn by over 15,000 men for an aggregate of approximately 400,000 man-hours. In addition to

personnel of the six American infantry divisions in Korea, other United Nations troops used the vest to a limited degree, including such specialised units as the helicopter pilots of 3rd Air Sea Rescue Squadron and the 8063rd, 8076th and 8209th Mobile Army Surgical Hospitals (MASH).

At the conclusion of Operation 'Boar' the body armour team presented its findings. The report stated:

'The Armor, Vest, Nylon, T-52-1 is much more effective against fragment type missiles than small arms missiles. During the test period, 67.9 per cent of all type missiles hitting the armor were defeated. 75.8 per cent of all fragments were defeated. 24.4 per cent of all small arms missiles were defeated. . . The Armor, Vest, Nylon, T-52-1, worn by soldiers in combat during the test period, reduced the incidence of chest and upper abdominal wounds by 60 to 70 per cent. It is estimated that 25 to 35 per cent of the chest and upper abdominal wounds sustained by combat soldiers wearing the armor during this test period were reduced in severity.'

The team also considered the psychological effects of the use of body armour and noted from interviews that, in actual combat, soldiers rarely noticed the weight and bulkiness of the vests. On the other hand, soldiers returning from uneventful patrols were more critical of its weight and limitation of mobility. However, over 85 per cent of troops stated that they felt safer and more confident when wearing body armour, a factor which led to higher morale and greater aggressiveness in combat.

On a few occasions its effect on morale was unfavourable, as when, for instance, soldiers who had previously used body armour expressed a reluctance to go on patrol without it. Indeed, the demand for the vest became so acute during one period of extremely heavy fighting that the test team members lost control of the study: soldiers who were wounded while wearing the vests were frequently relieved of their armour on the battlefield by their unprotected comrades. It is of interest to note that prior to Operation 'Boar' there were almost 10,000 of the earlier M12 type body armour held in depots in Korea but infrequently used. Following the operation and its attendant publicity, body armour was at such a premium that the supply of the M12 was rapidly exhausted.

During the test, recommendations based on combat experience for various modifications of the T-52-1 were forwarded to the United States, where they were incorporated into a new model, the *Armor, Vest, Nylon, T-52-2*. A total of 276 of the new vests were received in Korea on 9 July 1952 and were issued the following day. In the same month the body armour team returned to the United States. The T-52-3 prototype nylon armoured vest based on its recommendations was standardised in October 1952 as the *Armor, Vest, M-1952*. In a belated effort to provide its frontline troops with protection, the US Army ordered 13,020 Marine M-1951 vests on 11 August 1952. By 19 September 19,705 had been supplied, and this number steadily

Adorned in 'tiger stripe cammies', two Special Forces officers confer in a rice paddy near Nui Coto. Below his KKK scarf the helicopter pilot wears a ceramic/GRP 'chest protector'—Body Armor, Fragmentation—Small Arms Protective, Aircrewman. Designed to cover the front only for pilots and co-pilots, the 3713 series vest has a Nomex fire-retardant raschel-knit open back. The pocket on the front accommodates maps, pens, cigarettes, etc. Note the Nomex flying gloves, and the XM-177 Colt CAR-15 assault rifle. (Tim Page)

Clad in M-1955 armoured vests, typically worn open exposing chest and belly, a Marine mortar crew stand by their weapon on Hill 10 south of Da Nang. The M-1955 features a 3/4-collar and a rope ridge on the right shoulder to prevent a slung rifle from slipping; note the suspension webbing around the bottom of the vest. (Tim Page)

increased to approximately 63,000 by the time the Army vest was in production. The first shipment of the M-1952 was released in early December 1952, and by the end of hostilities approximately 26,161 vests of this type had been sent to Korea.

During the Korean War progress in combat medicine and surgery was so dramatic that the mortality rate among casualties wounded in action fell to 23 per 1,000 as compared to 45 per 1,000 in the Second World War. This reduction was due to several tactical innovations, of which the widespread use of body armour, coupled with helicopter evacuation of casualties to mobile army surgical hospitals and extensive use of whole blood were the most significant. One of the lucky survivors was a young subaltern of 1st Royal Tank Regiment, 1st Commonwealth Division, Lt. (later Lt.Col.) George Forty. On 28 May 1953, while Chinese artillery pounded the embattled 'Hook' position, he

The crew of a 'quad-fifty gun truck' prepare to move out on a convoy escort mission to Ban Me Thuot, September 1970. They are equipped with Variable Body Armor or, in its full designation, Variable Armor, Small Arms—Fragmentation Protective for Ground Troops. (US Army)

had to climb on to the hill in order to direct the fire of his Centurion tank against a hidden Chinese observation post. He recalls:

'As the shell fire was continuing I decided not only to wear a steel helmet, something which one didn't do very often, but also to put on the flak vest [M-1951] which was issued on the scale of one per tank. It was fortunately a fairly large one and so, because of my small stature, it covered rather more of me than on most people. However, it was bloody heavy.

'I started up the side of the 'Hook', but clearly I was being observed by the Chinese, and not long after they began to mortar me. Several rounds were fired, but the one that did the damage landed in the drainage ditch at the side of the track as I passed by. Fortunately I did not hear it coming, as I am quite sure I would have leapt into the ditch to take cover, so it would have landed on top of me. As it was, the blast was slightly contained and all I

remember is being hit by something like a sledgehammer on my legs which knocked me over.

'I tried to get to my feet, but found I could not do so; looking down at my legs I saw that they were covered in blood and that part of my left boot appeared to be missing. I was given morphine and, when a lull in the firing allowed, was taken by jeep to the Regimental Aid Post. Thereafter I went by helicopter post to an American MASH.

'As far as the flak vest was concerned it undoubtedly saved my life, because I had fragments in both my arms and both my legs up to the tops of my thighs but nothing penetrated my stomach or chest areas. The number of wounds to my arms and legs was considerable—indeed, I recall some 150 in all—but fortunately most of them were small fragments. By coincidence, there was also in the same ward a chap who had been on patrol and got sprayed by a Chinese burp gun; he had one bullet in his left arm, one in his right arm and a row of bruises across his chest, so clearly in his case the flak vest worked even better than for me!'

The Vietnam War

The Korean War demonstrated conclusively that a dramatic reduction in the incidence and severity of wounding was achieved by the use of body armour. Both the US Marine Corps and Army maintained post-war development of new fabrics and materials for a wide variety of tactical uses. Based on threat analysis and combat experience, both services introduced improved models incorporating a three-quarter collar of ballistic nylon for neck protection—the Marine *Vest, Armored, M-1955*; and, from 1962, the *Body Armor, Fragmentation Protective, Vest with $\frac{3}{4}$ Collar, M69*, for the Army. Together with the earlier M-1951 and M-1952 vests, these were the standard models of body armour used during the Vietnam War as protection against fragments.

The M-1955 was a sleeveless garment with a zipper front. The armour was made of nylon with 23 separate $5\frac{1}{4}$in. square, $\frac{1}{8}$in. thick Doron inserts in overlapping pockets below the shoulder area, which was formed by 13 layers of nylon as ballistic filler. The vest had a three-quarter collar made of six plies of ballistic nylon. The medium size weighed 10lbs 3oz, and cost $47.00.

The M69 vest contained a ballistic nylon filler sealed in a waterproof vinyl plastic casing. The filler consisted of 12 plies of ballistic nylon cloth in the front and upper back, ten plies in the back with an additional two plies, six inches wide, up the spine, and six plies in the collar. A set of plastic stiffeners was inserted under the fifth layer of ballistic nylon. The vest was encased in a layer of Oxford cloth, and incorporated into the outer shell were two pockets and grenade hanger loops. The vest had either a zipper or 'loop and pile' Velcro closure at the front, and elastic laces on each side. The medium size weighed 8lbs 5oz, and cost $35.00.

The proportion of deaths from small arms fire in

An Assault Support Patrol Boat settles by the stern after being hit by enemy fire in the Mekong Delta, June 1968. Wearing standard M-1952 and M69 flak jackets, the crew return fire while attempts are made to keep the craft afloat. (USN)

US Navy PBR (Patrol Boat River) crewmen examine the papers of Vietnamese aboard a sampan in the Mekong Delta. The two nearer men are wearing Body Armor, Fragmentation Protective, Titanium Nylon Composite. (USN)

South-East Asia, at 51 per cent, showed a marked increase over the Second World War (32 per cent) and Korea (33 per cent). This was due both to the nature of the war, and to the lethality of modern weapons of the rapid-fire M16/AK-47 type whose high-velocity, lightweight rounds caused severe tissue damage and increased risk of multiple wounding. However, hits from small arms fire decreased from 42.7 per cent in June 1966 to 16 per cent in June 1970, while the percentage from fragments (including mines and booby traps) rose from 49.6 per cent in 1966 to 80 per cent in 1970. The extensive use of mines and boobytraps in Vietnam resulted in appalling wounds, which because of the proximity of the blast caused massive local damage and hideous contamination from dirt, debris and secondary missiles impacted in the wounds.

Flak jackets did prove effective against three-quarters of the fragments which struck the thorax; but in the humid climate of Vietnam soldiers on the move often found the body armour too heavy and too hot. Troops in static positions and mechanised personnel usually wore both helmets and flak jackets; but infantry patrols, some unit commanders, and many individuals sacrificed protection, regardless of orders, in favour of greater mobility and reduced casualties from heat prostration. However, Marine Corps doctrine demanded that body armour be worn on all combat operations, even in the jungle with temperatures over 100°F. This fact is reflected in casualty data analysis which shows that 73 per cent of Marines wounded were wearing body armour at the time as against only 19 per cent for the Army.

One incident in December 1966 proved the wisdom of the Marine doctrine. While they were on a patrol in Quang Nam Province about 35 'klicks' south-west of Da Nang, a 155mm artillery round rigged as a tree mine exploded above a squad of Co. C, 1/1 Marines of 1st Marine Division. Seven men received terrible wounds, but thanks to the wearing of flak jackets and helmets there were no fatalities. One Marine had over 200 separate wounds to the buttocks, legs and arms but none to the head or torso. His M-1955 armoured vest was completely shredded, but it had performed its function—to provide protection against fragmentation projectiles.

As indicated above, body armour was worn less frequently by Army personnel, but on many occasions, the M69 proved to be just as effective, as in the case of Capt. A. Sambucchi when serving with 2nd Bn., 35th Artillery on 18 May 1969: 'An 82mm mortar burst about ten feet away. I sustained multiple fragment wounds in the arms, legs, face and head but none in the area covered by the vest. Later I was hit by a large fragment in the left side of the rib cage—fortunately the vest formed a seal for the sucking chest wound. The bunker caught fire and I suffered 2nd and 3rd degree burns, but again none on my torso.'

While neither the M-1955 nor M69 were designed to withstand small arms fire there were instances when the greater protection afforded by the Marine armoured vest proved itself: none more so than during the savage fighting for Hill 861A during the battle for Khe Sanh, when the forward positions of Co. E, 2/26 Marines were overrun by North Vietnamese sappers and assault troops. The Marines rapidly mounted a counter-attack which in the words of the 26th Marines Chronicle:

> . . . 'deteriorated into a mêlée that resembled a bloody, waterfront bar-room brawl: a style of fighting not completely alien to most Marines. Because the darkness and ground fog drastically reduced visibility, hand-to-hand combat was a necessity. Using their knives, bayonets rifle butts and fists, the men of 1st Platoon

1: British infantryman, 'Chemico'
   armour; Western Front, 1917
2: French infantryman, 'Lanciers'
   armour; Western Front, 1918
3: German assault infantryman,
   'Infanterie-Panzer' armour;
   Western Front, 1918

A

1: USAAF gunner, M1 & M4
   armour; Europe, 1944
2: British glider pilot,
   MRC armour; Arnhem, 1944
3: USAAF pilot, M2 & M5
   armour; Pacific, 1945

B

1: Turkish infantryman, M12 armour; Korea, 1953
2: US Marine, M-1951 armour; Korea, 1953
3: French Colonial Artilleryman, M-1952 armour; Dien Bien Phu, 1954

1: US Marine, M-1955 armour;
   Vietnam, 1968
2: US tank commander, M69 armour;
   Vietnam, 1968
3: US infantryman, 'Variable' armour;
   Vietnam, 1969

D

1: US Army helicopter crewman, 'chicken plate';
    Vietnam, 1970
2: US Navy gunner, 'Titanium/Nylon Composite' armour;
    Vietnam, 1969

1: British infantryman, M69 armour;
   Ulster, 1970s
2: British bomb disposal technician,
   EOD Mk.2 armour; Ulster, 1980s
3: British infantryman, late M69 armour;
   Ulster, 1980s

F

1: SWAT police officer, Second
   Chance Hardcorps 3 armour, 1980s
2: Trooper, 22 SAS Regt., BCME
   armour; Iranian Embassy, May 1980
3: Argentine Marine,
   Point Blank Mod.30 armour;
   Falklands, 1982

1: Israeli paratrooper, Rabintex RAV 200
    armour; Lebanon, 1982
2: US paratrooper, PASGT; Grenada, 1983
3: Soviet BMP commander, Afghanistan, 1984

ripped into the hapless North Vietnamese with a vengeance. Capt. Breeding [the company commander], a veteran of the Korean conflict who had worked his way up through the ranks, admitted that, at first, he was concerned over how his younger, inexperienced Marines would react in their first fight. As it turned out, they were magnificent. The captain saw one of his men come face to face with a North Vietnamese in the inky darkness; the young American all but decapitated his adversary with a crushing, round-house right to the face, then leaped on the flattened soldier and finished the job with a knife. Another man was jumped from behind by a North Vietnamese who grabbed him around the neck and was just about to slit his throat, when one of the Marine's buddies jabbed the muzzle of his M16 between the two combatants. With his selector on automatic, he fired off a full magazine; the burst tore huge chunks from the back of the embattled Marine's flak jacket but it also cut the North Vietnamese in half. Since the fighting was at such close quarters, both sides used hand grenades at extremely short range. The Marines had the advantage because of their armored vests and they would throw a grenade, then turn away from the blast, hunch up, and absorb the fragments in their flak jackets and the backs of their legs. On several occasions, Capt. Breeding's men used this technique and blew away enemy soldiers at less than ten metres.'

Aircrew armours

Although 80 per cent of wounds in Vietnam were caused by shell fragments, mines or boobytraps, the need arose to protect certain personnel such as helicopter crewmen from small arms fire. At the outset of Army aviation operations in Vietnam, crew members flew their support missions in H-21 Shawnee helicopters. The rotary-wing aircraft carried no armour and were relatively vulnerable to enemy fire. While crash-injury fatalities in aircraft hit by ground fire were three times those caused to crew members by bullet wounds, the Army Material Command initiated the Aircraft Armor Program in 1962 to reduce the vulnerability of Army aircraft and aircrewmen.

In 1918 the physicist, Maj. Neville Monroe Hopkins had concluded experimentally that even a $\frac{1}{16}$in. facing of hard enamel increased the armour protection of steel; but it was not until 1962 that this knowledge was exploited with the development of Hard Face Composite armour by Richard L. Cook of the Goodyear Aerospace Corporation, Akron, Ohio. The basic discovery demonstrated the effectiveness of armour combining a ceramic face with a backing of glass-reinforced plastic (GRP) against armour-piercing small arms rounds. When a bullet strikes the hard, brittle face of the ceramic, a conoid is formed in it which is projected by the bullet into the softer backing material. Since the area of the conoid base is much larger than the cross-sectional area of the bullet, energy is absorbed by the backing over a much wider area. During this instantaneous process the bullet is pulverised into fine particles by the ceramic armour, thus absorbing even more energy. The properties required of the ceramic are extreme hardness, to

To accommodate the smaller stature of ARVN soldiers a special version of the M69 flak jacket was made in reduced sizes and weights. It was classified as Body Armor, Fragmentation Protective for Vietnamese Forces. The medium size weighed 8.1lbs and cost $24.00. (*Infantry* **Magazine**)

At the outbreak of violence in Northern Ireland in 1969, British troops wore no protective armour except helmets. They were soon issued with standard US flak jackets. These soldiers are equipped for riot duty in 1969 with M-1952 vests, Mark 4 steel helmets, No. 4 Mark 2 respirators and wooden batons. (*Soldier Magazine*)

enable it to grind up the bullet; and low density, so that the ceramic layer is thick and the conoid has a large base area.

Ceramics such as aluminium oxide (Al_2O_3), silicon carbide (SiC) and boron carbide (B_4C) are commonly used. Boron carbide, in particular, which is the third hardest material known to man after diamond and borazon, is an outstanding armour material. Ceramics, however, are difficult and therefore expensive to manufacture; they are brittle, and will often crack or shatter if dropped; and although capable of absorbing multiple strikes without penetration, they have to be replaced after being hit.

In 1962, as part of the Aircraft Armor Program, 'personnel protective armor kits' were supplied for the various Army aircraft operating in the Republic of Vietnam. Critical aircraft components and personnel positions were protected by a

'Doron/Perforating-Steel/Tipping Plate armor kit' and aircrewmen were provided with a protective vest incorporating individual 6in. square ceramic/GRP plates inserted into cloth pockets. The plates wore through the pockets, however, and there was no ballistic protection at the seams. In consequence these vests were rarely worn, and the usual body armour for aircrewmen at this time was the standard M-1952 fragmentation vest. While they were effective against shattered plexiglass and spall from the structure of aircraft hit by ground fire, many aircrewmen also believed that the vest provided protection from small arms fire. It was not uncommon for the chin bubble of helicopters to be filled with vests, obscuring the pilot's downward vision, and for crewchiefs and gunners to stand on layer of fragmentation vests sewn together and placed on the cargo compartment floor as a 'flak carpet'. Helicopter aircrewmen favoured the M-1952 vest rather than the M69 because the collar of the latter interfered with the flight helmet.

By 1965 the UH-1 'Huey' was the principal helicopter used on combat operations in Vietnam. At this time, the aircraft was fitted with a 'Hard Face Composite (HFC) armor kit' incorporating interchangeable armoured/unarmoured seats for the pilot and co-pilot which gave ballistic protection from 7.62mm/.30cal. AP rounds on the seat bottom, sides and back. The armoured seat was composed of a continuous-wall boron carbide armoured bucket laminated with fibreglass. As part of the HFC kit two chest protectors were provided for the pilot and co-pilot. These replaced the earlier separate plate protective vests, and were made by bonding 13 ceramic tiles to a fibreglass-reinforced shell which extended from the collarbone to the groin. The shield was shaped at the bottom to clear the thighs, enabling its $18\frac{1}{2}$lb weight to rest on the pilot's seat by an extension at the groin. In practice the chest protectors invariably cut into the pilot thighs, causing such extreme personal discomfort and restriction of movement that they were rarely used.

During early 1965 a team of Army Material Command personnel visited Vietnam to address the problems of aircraft and aircrew armour protection. In order to make immediate use of the approximately 500 'HFC armor chest protectors' then on hand in Vietnam, the team devised an interim solution to the problem of frontal torso protection by cutting three inches off the bottom of the chest protectors and encasing them in cloth back carriers. The work was undertaken by the ARVN 92nd Aerial Equipment Repair and Depot Company, and the modified chest protector was known as the 'T65-1 frontal torso armor'. This item proved to be acceptable to aircrewmen, as did an experimental three-section, rigid front ceramic torso armour developed by the team during its time in Vietnam.

On the team's return to the United States, a standardised item classified as *Body Armor, Small Arms Protective, Aircrewman* was developed for helicopter gunners and crewchiefs who needed back and front protection. For pilots and co-pilots who sat in armoured seats and required only frontal protection, the *Body Armor, Small Arms Protective, Aircrewman, Front Plate with Carrier for Pilot and Co-Pilot* was provided. Three types of ceramic were used: Class I Al_2O_3, Class II SiC and Class III modified B_4C. Class I was used only by the Army while Classes II and III were used by the Navy, Air Force and Marine Corps. They ranged in weight and cost from Al_2O_3 regular size at $28\frac{1}{2}$lbs and $195.00 to modified B_4C at $20\frac{3}{4}$lbs and $1,018.00.

All these body armours incorporated monolithic ceramic plates rather than individual tiles, thus eliminating the ballistic weakness of joints between them and spreading the shock wave from the projectile over a greater area. The single ceramic plate was less expensive to produce than a mosaic of multiple tiles which had to be bevelled at the edges (to maintain the desired ballistic level) and carefully cemented to the supporting fibreglass shell. During 1966 and 1967 over 20,000 items of aircrew armour were supplied to South-East Asia.

The aircrewman's body armour proved highly effective against 7.62mm/.30cal. AP rounds; but on occasion, blindness and other collateral damage resulted from the splash and spall issuing off the front of the ceramic armour when struck by bullets, as in the case of WO1 Maurice H. Richey, an assault helicopter pilot of the 134th Aviation Company. On 17 November 1969 the lower right side of his armour plate was hit by a .30cal. bullet from about 500 feet range. The pilot sustained only a bruise on the torso, but the ricochet tore away a large piece of his right bicep.

From 1968 this problem was overcome by the

Purpose-designed riot equipment for the troops in Northern Ireland was quickly developed, such as these Anti-Riot Leg Protectors; previously, copies of *Playboy* or other magazines were stuffed down trouser legs to protect against hand-thrown missiles. Note the 3/4-collar of the M69 vest (right) as compared to the M-1952 (left), from which the shoulder straps have been removed to prevent rioters from grasping them. Note also the S6 respirators strapped to these Royal Greenjackets' left arms. (*Soldier* **Magazine**)

introduction of the *Body Armor, Fragmentation—Small Arms protective, Aircrewman*, which thereafter became the standard issue item. It incorporated the same three types of ceramic inserts, but they were covered with ballistic nylon and their carrying pockets were lined with nylon felt which entrapped any spall or fragments caused by an impacting projectile. This certainly worked for SP4 Charles W. Smith of the 242nd Assault Support Helicopter Company. On 25 April 1968, Smith, while acting as a gunner in a CH-47 Chinook, was hit in the centre of his front armour plate by an AK-47 round. The round lodged halfway through the armour and the impact propelled Smith across the helicopter. He remained unconscious for several minutes, but sustained no other injuries.

In addition to torso protection, the Army

A 'Greenfinch' of the Ulster Defence Regt. swaps her beret for a Black Watch bonnet prior to VCP duty in Northern Ireland. These flak jackets, both M-1952 and M69, are fitted with British-made protective covers featuring straight pockets and both snap-fastener and Velcro closures. These are second-pattern covers with a rubber non-slip rifle-rest on the right shoulder face; the first-pattern has no patches, and the third, patches on each shoulder. (MoD)

were delivered to Vietnam in February 1966—see Plate E1.

Like the mounted knight of the Middle Ages, whose horse gave him mobility despite his great weight of armour, the Vietnam combat aircrewman rode to battle in his helicopter. Just as the knight was the aristocrat of war and equipped with expensive armour, the aircrewman flew encased in thousands of dollars' worth of protection—a luxury justified by the expense of training him and the huge replacement cost of his aircraft. Between 1962 and 1968 there were 4,065 casualties (including 478 fatalities) among Army aircrewmen, and from 1968 through to 1970 there were 8,250 casualties, including 1,499 fatalities. From wound data analysis, it is estimated that aircrew armour prevented 23 per cent of wounds and 49 per cent of fatal wounds during the first period, and 27 per cent and 53 per cent during the second. While wounds outnumbered injuries by two to one, fatal injuries—the majority in crashes with fire—outnumbered fatal wounds by five to two. Hence, although aircrew armour was highly effective and prevented an estimated 3,403 fatal and non-fatal wounds up to 1970, it is evident that extensive armouring of personnel has limitations in the reduction of overall fatal casualties. Furthermore, the real penalty for armouring the helicopter and/or its crew is less time in the air per sortie or reduced ordnance/payload.

* * *

The success of aircrew armour gave rise to a similar demand for protecting the ground soldier against small arms fire. It was not possible to provide equivalent protection without impeding his effectiveness, and considerable materials research was necessary to provide even near parity. It will be noted that the original ceramic for aircrew armour was aluminium oxide (Al_2O_3); but with the introduction of boron carbide, equivalent protection could be provided with a weight reduction of 20 per cent. This was sufficient to make a comparable body armour for infantry feasible. It was classified as *Variable Armor, Small Arms-Fragmentation Protective, for Ground Troops*, or simply 'Variable Body Armor'. Some 40,000 were manufactured in 1968, and it was employed in Vietnam from the following year.

Variable Body Armor consisted of an outer shell of ballistic nylon cloth with a ballistic filler of

developed full-leg armour for gunners and crew-chiefs; pilots and co-pilots used their legs and feet too much in flight operations to tolerate the extra burden. Between 1962 and 1970 leg wounds represented 27.5 per cent of the total hits but resulted in only 18 airborne fatalities. The armour consisted of frontal thigh and lower leg units which were joined by an articulating hinge at the knee. It was constructed from dual-hardness steel as well as ceramics and weighed approximately 38lbs per pair. Designed to provide protection against 7.62mm/.30cal. AP projectiles, the first 500 pairs of dual-hardness composite steel full-leg armour

The commander of the British Force in Lebanon and his armoured car crew stand guard on the roof of the apartment block which served as the BRITFORLEB base in Beirut. These flak jackets have the fifth-pattern cover with PVC patches on each shoulder; the previous model had a single patch on the right shoulder only. Note the Velcro 'loop and pile' closure of these jackets. The berets are (left) 16th/5th The Queen's Royal Lancers; (centre, right) Prince of Wales's Own Yorkshire Regiment. (Nat. Army Mus.)

needle-punched nylon felt. At the front and back were large pockets to accommodate anatomically shaped ceramic/GRP composite armour plates. The plates had an integral carrier system of webbing and straps allowing them to be worn independently of the vest. Thus the vest could be worn without plates (giving protection against fragments only), with front plate only, or with both front and back plates. Additionally, the plates could be worn without the vest, providing either front only or front and back protection against .30cal. ball projectiles. The 'Five-Way Variable Armor System'—see Plate D3—offered the user a wide choice of options in the level of protection to match operational requirements and the anticipated threat, at a system weight ranging from 5lbs 4oz to 22lbs 3oz and a unit cost of $385.00.

In Vietnam, the Navy and Coastguard fought a vicious type of warfare patrolling the extensive coastline and inland waterways in a variety of attack craft. Constantly exposed to mines and ambushes, their casualties were high and unremitting. M-1955 and M69 fragmentation vests were used, but they did not float, and when worn with life jackets they restricted movement due to their excessive bulk. A floating body armour was finally developed called *Vest Buoyant, Ballistic, Fragmentation—Small Arms, Protective*, but the 'Brown Water Navy's' part in the war had ended before it was standardised. At 28lbs it was heavy and bulky; but the present author, a non-swimmer, can attest that it floats!

Many 'riverine' personnel made use of a body armour that was in limited use by the Army and by Navy Special Forces SEAL teams, known as *Body Armor, Fragmentation Protective, Titanium/Nylon Composite*. Developed in 1964, this armour consisted of $2\frac{1}{4}$in. square by 0.032in. thick titanium plates and four plies of ballistic nylon. Increased mobility was provided by dividing the vest into eleven sections, each consisting of three plies of ballistic nylon covered by a series of titanium plates, and by incorporating an articulated pivot shoulder similar in design to a gridiron football player's shoulder pad. Weighing 8lbs 11oz, it cost $174.00, and gave comparable protection against fragments to the M1 helmet, together with increased protection against flechettes—see Plate E2.

Many other items of protective equipment were developed during the Vietnam War, ranging from blast-protective boots to fire-resistant Nomex flying uniforms, and from polycarbonate face shields to ballistic flight helmets. For every threat, American ingenuity devised a counter measure—a graphic example being *pungi* stakes. This simple device comprised mantraps sown with sharpened bamboos or nails, often smeared with excrement to cause infection, which could penetrate the soles of the standard combat and jungle boots. The counter was equally simple, and took the form of a removable spike-resistant insole made from several layers of Saran screen fabric cemented to a plastic-covered stainless steel sheet. It was introduced into Vietnam from August 1965, and from May 1966 the tropical combat boot was manufactured with the steel insert moulded directly into the sole.

An EOD (Explosive Ordnance Disposal) Ammunition Technician (AT) examines an IED (Improvised Explosive Device) which he has disabled by means of a 'Wheelbarrow' Remote Handling Device. One of the most sophisticated (and heaviest) forms of body armour, the EOD Mark 2 suit provides a measure of blast and fragment protection against bomb explosions; or, in the words of one AT, 'at least it enables you to be buried in one piece!' (Simon Dunstan)

Modern Body Armour

Kevlar: Police initiatives

The basis of all modern 'soft' body armour is an aramid fibre known as Kevlar. First discovered in 1965 by the Du Pont Company, it was originally engineered to reinforce radial tyres and rubber goods such as hoses and conveyor belts. The synthetic aramid fibre has a specific tensile strength five times higher than that of the strongest steel wire and three times that of nylon. Early in the 1970s the US Army Materials and Mechanics Research Center (AMMRC), Watertown, Massachusetts, determined that Kevlar had outstanding powers of ballistic resistance. AMMRC and the US Army Natick Laboratories initiated programmes to develop Kevlar fabrics for flak jackets, and research was also undertaken to use it in reinforced plastic helmets.

Although the initial development emphasised fragmentation resistance, it was also discovered that Kevlar had the ability to arrest a wide assortment of handgun projectiles at significantly less weight than ballistic nylon cloth. Learning this, Lester Shubin, programme manager for standards of the National Institute of Law Enforcement and Criminal Justice (NILECJ), realised its potential for police body armour. At that time the only items available were military flak jackets, whose bulk and protective characteristics were unsuited to police work. Du Pont provided a few pounds of Kevlar, which was then in very short supply. At a firing range at the Aberdeen Proving Ground, Maryland, 100 goats were dressed in Kevlar vests less than half an inch thick and then, in what might have struck a passer-by as a depraved ritual, marksmen fired at them with .22 and .38cal. pistols—the weapons police are most likely to encounter on the streets. All the goats survived, and suffered nothing worse than bruises.

Following these trials, an extensive research and development programme was initiated to develop bullet-resistant vests for police officers. Several fabric styles were developed and one, a balanced plain weave made from 1,000 denier yarns of Kevlar 29, was shown to have an excellent combination of ballistic performance and light weight. Tests indicated that by combining five layers of this fabric, a vest could be made which would stop a typical .38 Special round (158-grain Round-Nose Soft-Point at 800 feet/second) or a .22, 40-grain RNSP round at 1,000 feet/second. Seven layers could stop a 230-grain .45 Automatic round, and 28 layers, a .44 Magnum round. Fitted with a waterproof, opaque outer covering (the ballistic performance of Kevlar is degraded if wet or exposed to sunlight) and non-metallic straps and fasteners to avoid secondary missiles), a five-ply vest weighed only $1\frac{1}{2}$lbs, while protecting the wearer in the front and back torso areas. Furthermore, the vest was concealable and comfortable enough to wear on a full-time basis.

In 1975, 5,000 seven-layer Kevlar vests were distributed to 15 police departments throughout the United States. During the first year five police officers wearing vests were assaulted, two with handguns, two with knives and one with a heavy wooden club. None was seriously injured. The first incident occurred on 23 December 1975 when Ray Johnson, a Seattle patrolman, was standing in a checkout line at a supermarket while off duty but in uniform. During the course of a robbery he was shot in the chest with a .38 revolver. Lester Shubin recounts: 'He was shot from only three feet away and he didn't even fall down, so the guy shot him again. We rushed out to Seattle to see him. All he had under the vest was two mean-looking bruises. He was out of hospital in three days.' Two other officers who were issued vests but chose not to wear them were assaulted with handguns and received serious wounds.

While the requisite number of layers of Kevlar will stop bullets, the energy of the impact can cause severe but non-lethal injuries—an effect known as 'blunt trauma'. This can be minimised by extra layers of Kevlar or by the addition of shock-absorbing material behind the armour. When a fibre is struck by a projectile it stretches and transmits energy along its length. The greater the length of fibre affected, the better the ballistic resistance. Because Kevlar has the greatest 'effective' length of any textile fibre, it has the ability both to defeat projectiles and to dissipate the impact energy over a wide area, thus reducing the effect of blunt trauma.

In July 1976 a Nashville patrol officer, driving to an emergency call, sped over a hill to find an 18-wheeler tractor/trailer rig slewed across the road. In

A member of a Royal Engineer Search Team uses his No. 6 Mine Prod to scrutinise an empty bag of fertilizer—one of the constituents of IRA 'Co-op mix' bombs—in a farm outhouse near the Irish border. He is wearing 'US Variable Body Armour' with ceramic plates, front and rear, and an ART helmet. Search teams now use a range of purpose-designed body armour items, including a special helmet incorporating communications equipment. (*Soldier* **Magazine**)

the ensuing collision the impact forced the police car's bumper to the firewall, and the shattered steering column hit the officer in the chest. On account of his body armour he sustained only bruising in what would otherwise have been a fatal accident.

Wearing Kevlar body armour also provides a degree of protection against knife slashes, but not against the direct thrust of a sharp, pointed weapon such as a stiletto. To every rule, however, there is an exception—as in the case of Officer Eva Rosenblatt of the Baltimore Metropolitan Police Department, who was struck in the breasts with an ice pick. Her protective vest prevented penetration, and she shot her assailant dead.

In 1974 a total of 132 federal, state and local officers were killed in the line of duty in the United States. All but four were the victims of firearms. Ninety-five of them were killed by handguns, the most common being .38, .32, .25 and .22cal. models. These weapons represent 80 per cent of all confiscated firearms in the US and 90–95 per cent of the country's private handgun arsenal. After the widespread introduction of body armour in 1975, fatalities were reduced to 94 in 1978, and have

Policemen of the Royal Ulster Constabulary (RUC) on patrol wearing Bristol Grade 25 Armour, manufactured by Bristol Composite Materials Engineering Limited (BCME). This was the first body armour model to see widespread service with British police forces. Note the lack of side protection. (RUC)

remained at around 100 ever since even though the assault rate has risen. Since 1975 over 500 law enforcement officers in the US have been saved from death or serious injury from a variety of weapons by their body armour. Law enforcement agencies throughout the world now use Kevlar vests, as do VIPs and celebrities—the reason Secretary of State Henry Kissinger wore a full-length trench coat throughout his Middle East diplomacy missions was that it was lined with Kevlar, as are former President Gerald Ford's golfing jackets.

Military Developments

In the final days of America's involvement in Vietnam, the US Army developed a lighter version of the M69 to overcome the menace of heat exhaustion. Body armour forms an impervious barrier, preventing heat-loss by moisture evaporation, and while this may be desirable in cold climates it places a severe heat load on troops in hot ones. Designated *Body Armor, Lightweight, Fragmentation Protective Vest with ¾ Collar, M-71N*, the new armour was made of ballistic nylon and featured articulated shoulder pads for greater flexibility. It was not adopted because of a Joint Operational Requirement for a vest for both the Army and Marine Corps weighing only 5lbs but with the same protection level as the M69. The Army's Natick Research and Development Command produced a modified vest standardised in 1975 as the *Body*

Armor, Fragmentation Protective Vest (ICM)—Improved Conventional Munitions.

The ICM vest consists of 12 layers of surface-resistant treated ballistic nylon, eliminating the need for a waterproof vinyl pouch. To provide for mobility, the back is made in four sections. The three upper ones slide over each other and over the lower back section to allow for any changes in body dimensions associated with various movements. Shoulder pads with elastic webbing and snap fasteners allow more freedom of arm movement independent of the rest of the vest. The overlapping front and back protect the sides, and elastic webbing allows for movement and size adjustment. The three-quarter collar is flexible enough to be worn turned up or down and is designed for increased fragmentation protection to the neck and throat areas. Produced in four sizes, the outer layer of the vest comes in a camouflage pattern or in Navy and Olive Drab colours. The ICM is one pound lighter than the M69, and its bulk is 25 per cent less, which makes it more compatible with weapons and equipment in use.

With the refinement of Kevlar as a ballistic material, the vest is now manufactured incorporating the aramid fibre in accordance with Military Specification LP/P DES 19-77A dated 26 April 1978. The ballistic filler consists of 14oz WR (water repellant) Treated Kevlar. The inner and outer shell of the vest is WR Treated 8oz ballistic nylon cloth. Weighing 9lbs in the medium size, it is designated *Body Armor, Fragmentation Protective Vest Ground Troops (PASGT)—Personal Armor System for Ground Troops*. It is the current body armour worn by the US Armed Forces. As a part of PASGT a new helmet was introduced in 1982 designated *Helmet, Ground Troops—Parachutists (PASGT)*. It is made of Kevlar and a plastic (phenolic modified polyvinyl butyral) at 20 per cent of total weight to provide rigidity. On account of its similarity in appearance to the classic German helmet it has been nicknamed the 'Fritz', and is credited with saving the lives of at least two troopers of the 82nd Airborne Division during the invasion of Grenada—see Plate H2.

In the British Army, despite its successful use in the Korean War, body armour is only sanctioned for wear during internal security duties. Soon after the start of the 'Troubles' in Northern Ireland in

1969, troops were equipped with standard M-1952 and M69 flak jackets. These were subsequently fitted with a series of British-made protective covers. Troops now wear a discreet garment of greatly increased capability known as *Improved Northern Ireland Body Armour (INIBA)* or *Mark 2 Body Armour*. Due to this disjunction in operational doctrine, few soldiers in the Falkland Islands campaign of 1982 wore flak jackets. It must be admitted that the 'footslogging' nature of the fighting argued against their use by already cruelly burdened infantry. Again, most battalion attacks were launched against entrenched and fortified positions, so the majority of casualties were caused by small arms fire: at the battle for Darwin and Goose Green 58 per cent of all fatal and non-fatal casualties were due to gunshot wounds with the remainder to fragmentation weapons. Even so, it is arguable that some of the latter could have been avoided by using body armour.

The Falklands War did see the first operational employment of helicopter aircrew body armour in the British Armed Forces. Twenty-two sets of Noroc 1 Armor Systems were deployed during Operation 'Corporate'—fabricated from boron carbide cera-

mic backed by reinforced plastic laminates, they are produced by the Norton Company of Worcester, Massachusetts. Fifteen sets sailed on HMS *Intrepid* and seven on the *Atlantic Conveyor*; four of the latter were lost when she was sunk by an Exocet. Two sets were worn in action in the one remaining HC-1 Chinook, 'Bravo November' of No. 18 Sqn. RAF, by its two pairs of pilots. The Norton body armour was worn for a total of 1,310 hours during Operation 'Corporate', but no hits were sustained.

Today's ballistic resistant vests of the 'soft' armour type contain up to 40 layers of Kevlar, and are designed to protect the torso against a high proportion of fragments from exploding artillery shells, grenades and other explosive devices, as well as low-velocity handgun and sub-machine gun ammunition. Kevlar is suitable for use against fragments with impact velocities of up to 1,000 metres/second and against bullets up to 550 metres/second. Since the actual energy of a projectile depends on numerous factors such as barrel length, the type of round and propellant, body armour must be custom-designed to meet the anticipated threat.

To take an example of the problem which designers may face, the Soviet 7.62mm rimless pistol round has a muzzle velocity of 420 metres/second when fired from the Soviet Tokarev TT Model 1938 pistol; but Tokarev 7.62mm cartridges manufactured in Czechoslovakia carry a heavier load, so the 7.62mm Czech Model 52 pistol has a muzzle velocity of 490 metres/second. Even the standard Soviet-issue round can achieve still higher velocities given a longer barrel. Fired from the PPSh M1941 sub-machine gun of Second World War fame, this round can develop velocities of up to 500 metres/second. Furthermore, although many armies employ pistols or sub-machine guns of 9mm calibre, the number of Kevlar plies required to thwart Parabellum Gecko ammunition is greater than that required to stop UK Mk.2Z ammunition, and Norma Luger 19022 ammunition requires even more. It is up to the user to specify the exact threat so that the armour designer can work to this goal. Protection against rifle bullets and armour-piercing small arms rounds generally requires approximately seven times as much weight per unit area as that used in fragmentation jackets, and any

A Special Patrol Group of the RUC dash to their Hotspur armoured Land Rovers at Musgrave Street police station in Belfast. Current body armour equipment includes these Bristol Body Armour Type 1 jackets and anti-riot helmets. (RUC)

The gamut of commercially-produced equipment currently available to policemen presents a daunting picture in the year 1984. This figure displays an ARH83 helmet and visor, Riot Leg Shields, NR82 Respirator with integral speech diaphragm, Nomex fire-retardant coveralls, and SES Type Combat Vest made of Kevlar; it has an optional chest pocket for insertion of a ceramic plate for protection against high-velocity bullets. He is armed with a Schermuly 38mm Anti-Riot Gun, a 26in. beech riot baton and a handgun. (Eric Ford—Security Equipment Supplies Ltd)

fabric armour would be excessively bulky. Specially prepared steel plates (see Plate G1) or ceramics, weighing approximately 20lbs, are currently used against this threat; but much lighter combinations of metal alloys and Kevlar are now in the development stages, and promise to equal or surpass the performance of these units.

In 5,000 years body armour has progressed from fabric and leather to bronze, then to steel, and now back to fabric. These developments have not been governed entirely by the need for defence against the improved penetrating power of modern weapons. The flak jackets described here cannot yet defeat either the high-velocity rifle rounds of today, or the arrows of a millenium or more ago. Even the spears of ancient warriors could penetrate current body armour; but the science of warfare has changed radically, and the hazards posed by the predominance of fragmentation munitions demand the use of lightweight vests which are capable of defeating most of these fragments. A synthesis of battle casualty analysis in the 20th century reveals that over two-thirds of all wounds have been due to fragments. Modern body armour can prevent many of these, and can reduce chest and abdominal wounds by up to three-quarters.

Body armour does not make a modern soldier invulnerable to contemporary weapons; but helmets and fragmentation vests can and must be worn in almost all military circumstances. The protection of troops in a society that places a high value on individual life is a humane necessity, and is all the more desirable when this protection is inexpensive and practical. In terms of harsh military reality, any item that can prevent losses of the expensively trained soldiers of the small, professional armies of today is a positive investment. The wide range of body armour now available offers a simple method of preserving life and reducing the severity of combat injuries.

The Plates

A1: British infantry 'bomber' with Chemico Body Shield; Western Front, 1917

'Bombers' were troops specially trained for trench fighting, taking their title from their principal weapon, the Mills Bomb. This soldier is equipped for a trench raid with bombs and a 'morningstar' club made up from a polo ball studded with .303 bullets. He is dressed in a Chemico Body Shield with groin protector, principally to protect himself from fragments of his own bombs when fighting at close quarters. This particular Chemico belonged to Cpl. Sidney W. Cooper of the 2/6th North Staffordshire Regiment.

A2: French 'poilu' with Lanciers cuirass; Western Front, 1918

Acting as a sentinel, a 'poilu' stands guard in a 'Lanciers' cuirass of overlapping steel plates. As protection for the head and face, his 'casque Adrian' is fitted with the third-pattern 'visière système Polack', designed by Médecin Aide-Major Polack,

hich saw limited service towards the end of the
reat War. His other equipment is standard
rench issue, including the 'bidon modèle 1872'
anteen) at his side for 'pinard', the thin red wine
sential to sustain the 'poilu', or, if he is lucky, the
w, fiery liquor—'gniole'.

*3: German 'Stosstrupp' with Infanterie-Panzer; Western
Front, 1918*
lthough it was rarely worn in the assault because
' its weight, some German soldiers, particularly
renadiers', did attire themselves in 'Sap-
enpanzer' during attacks and raids. This member
' an élite 'Sturmkompanie' assault party has the
ter model which incorporated refinements such as
e rifle rest on the right shoulder and equipment
)oks on the breastplate. His helmet is the 1918
odel issued in the closing months of the war.

*1: USAAF B-17 'Flying Fortress' waist gunner with
Flyer's Armor; European Theatre of Operations, 1944*
ver his electrically heated flying outfit, this .50cal.
rowning gunner is wearing a 'flak suit' comprising
yer's Armor Vest M1 providing front and back
rotection; Flyer's Armor Apron M4 attached to
e front of the M1 vest by three quick release
steners; and Helmet M4 consisting of segments of
adfield steel in overlapping cloth pockets.

*2: British sergeant, Glider Pilot Regiment with MRC
Body Armour; Operation 'Market Garden', Arnhem,
1944*
)dy armour was rarely worn by ground troops
iring the Second World War. Expected to fight as
1 infantryman once on the ground, this sergeant
the Glider Pilot Regt. displays the Medical
esearch Council Body Armour.

*3: USAAF B-29 'Superfortress' pilot with Flyer's
Armor; Pacific Theatre of Operations, 1945*
y 1945 'flak suits' were in widespread use by the
S Army Air Forces. This bomber pilot is encased
Flyer's Armor Vest M2; Flyer's Groin Armor
I5, with a skirt over each thigh and a centre-piece
)on which he sits; and Helmet M5.

*1: Turkish infantryman with Armor, Vest, M12; Korea,
1953*
lade up for the most part of volunteers, the

With blood streaming down his face from a headwound
caused by a bullet that penetrated his helmet, an Israeli soldier
wearing an M69 vest tends a wounded companion during an
Egyptian attack near the Suez Canal, 6 November 1969. The
Israeli Army first procured body armour on a large scale
during the War of Attrition, 1967–70. (IDF)

Turkish Brigade gained a fearsome reputation in
Korea. This soldier is kitted out entirely with US
equipment including an Armor, Vest, M12.

*C2: US Marine with Vest, Armored, M-1951; Korea,
1953*
One of several significant tactical and technical
innovations instituted by the US Marine Corps
during the Korean War was the 'flak vest' in the
form of the Vest, Armored, M-1951, as shown on
this rifleman.

*C3: Caporal, French Colonial Artillery, with Armor, Vest,
M-1952; Indo-China, April/May 1954*
During the battle of Dien Bien Phu, several
consignments of American flak jackets were
parachuted into the beleaguered garrison to protect
artillerymen and other personnel fighting in fixed
positions. This Senegalese corporal of 4/II/4ᵉ
RAC is serving a 105mm howitzer at strongpoint
'Claudine' in an Armor, Vest, M-1952, during the
last days of the siege.

*D1: US Marine with Vest, Armored, M-1955; Vietnam,
1968*
This Marine hurling a grenade is depicted in the

35

Israeli soldiers scan Syrian positions from a military post in the Beka'a Valley, October 1982. They are wearing the first-pattern Israeli-produced flak jacket made of Kevlar. Flak jackets were worn extensively by the Israeli Army during the invasion of Lebanon in 1982, so much so that some military observers dubbed it the 'War of the Vest'. (IDF)

battle of Hue during the Tet offensive of 1968. His Vest, Armored, M-1955 is adorned with typical slogans—against regulations, which allowed only name and number to be inscribed on flak jackets and helmets.

D2: US tank commander with Body Armor, Fragmentation Protective, Vest with ¾ Collar, M69; Vietnam, 1968
Over his jungle fatigues, this TC of 11th Armored Cavalry Regt. is wearing an M69 flak vest surmounted by a Combat Vehicle Crewman's (CVC) helmet with integral communications; composed of plastic resin-coated ballistic nylon, it gives almost equivalent protection as the M1 helmet.

D3: US infantryman with Variable Armor, Small Arms—Fragmentation Protective, for Ground Troops; Vietnam, 1969
The US 9th Div. fought a grim and gruelling campaign among the Rung Sat swamps and the Mekong Delta waterways. As a point man on patrol, this 'Old Reliable' is wearing Variable Body Armor; M1 helmet; and the experimental quick-drying 'Delta Boots' to offset dermatophytosis

(trench foot)—another example of special protective clothing devised for the combat soldier.

E1: US Army aviator with Body Armor and Leg Armor, Small Arms Protective, Aircrewman; Vietnam, 1970
Laying down suppressive fire, a crewchief leans far out of his Huey helicopter, protected from enemy fire by ceramic body and composite-steel leg armour. The body armour was commonly called 'chicken plate' as a reflection on the wearer's courage. The inset view shows the front of the earlier 'T65-1 frontal torso armor', with a crude bullseye painted on it as an act of bravura; and the rear of the standard item embellished with typical graffito of the period.

E2: US Navy PBR gunner with Body Armor, Fragmentation Protective, Titanium/Nylon Composite; Vietnam, 1969
The flak jacket of this front gunner on a Patrol Boat River plying the Ca Mao is liberally decorated with bellicose comments: below the articulated shoulder pads is written SAT CONG—'Kill Communists'; LINE LOI is that classic statement of the Vietnam War—'Sorry About That'; and SIN LOI does not bear translation. The configuration of American footballers' protective clothing and helmets has had a significant influence on body armour design; conversely, a torso protector worn by some quarterbacks is commonly referred to as a 'flak jacket' because of their dangerous rôle on the gridiron football field.

F1: British infantryman with Fragmentation Vest; Ulster, 1970s
The British Army has devised numerous items of body armour and protective devices to meet the exigencies of the internal security campaign in Northern Ireland. Attired for riot control, this soldier wears an M69 flak jacket with third-pattern protective cover; Anti-Riot Leg Protectors; and an Anti-Riot Topper (ART) helmet, known to troops as the 'Cromwell' after the name of the manufacturers—it was originally to be designated Fragmentation, Anti-Riot, Topper, but the acronym was deemed unseemly. He is further protected by a polycarbonate 'Makrolon' shield and is armed with a Schermuly 38mm Anti-Riot Gun.

2: British bomb disposal technician with EOD Mark 2 Suit; Ulster, 1980s

Attached to 321 Explosive Ordnance Disposal Company, 'The Bang Gang', this Ammunition Technician is partially protected against bomb blast and fragmentation by the EOD Mark 2 Suit and EOD Mark 3 Helmet. The suit incorporates rigid armour breast and pelvic plates with separate Kevlar jacket and trousers. Weighing 42lbs, it is worn for only short periods when the AT is actually inspecting a suspect device.

3: British infantryman with Fragmentation Vest; Ulster, 1980s

Besides the standard DPM uniform, this soldier on foot patrol has a 'skeleton' webbing consisting of ammunition pouches, two water-bottles, and a poncho liner 'bum roll' with a damp towel wrapped inside to offset petrol and acid bomb attack. His M69 has the last pattern British cover incorporating field dressing pouch on the right shoulder and pocket fasteners for a two-way radio-phone. In British service the M69 and M-1952 are designated simply 'Fragmentation Vest' or alternatively, 'Flak Jacket'; troops are currently equipped with a discreet body armour worn under the combat smock.

G1: SWAT team member with Second Chance Hardcorps 3 Body Armor; a US metropolitan police department, 1980s

Special Weapons and Tactics (SWAT) teams are equipped to meet the most dire situations in the law enforcement field. Slightly heavier, but more robust, than ceramics, the laminated steel alloy plates of the Hardcorps 3 body armour are capable of stopping 7.62×51 NATO AP rounds at 100 metres and all Soviet 7.62×39 'AK-47' rounds at point blank range: sufficient to defeat nearly all weapons in the hands of criminals or terrorists. This trooper is armed with a Mossberg 500-ATP-8SP pump-action shotgun; his German Shepherd 'K-9' companion is protected by an Armoured Dog Jacket which is resistant to .38 Special rounds.

USAF security police form a cordon at Ramstein Air Force Base as demonstrators protest against the deployment of Intermediate Range Nuclear Missiles, August 1983. This view gives a good comparison between the M69 (centre) and the current US Armed Forces PASGT body armour. (USAF)

US Marines patrol 'Sandbag City', the Marine compound at Beirut Airport in the Lebanon, November 1983. They are wearing Body Armor, Fragmentation Protective Vest, Ground Troops (PASGT)—Personal Armor System for Ground Troops. (USMC)

G2: SAS Trooper with BCME Variable Armour; 'Pagoda' Troop, CRW Team, 22nd Special Air Service Regiment; Operation 'Nimrod', Iranian Embassy, 5 May 1980

The SAS are allowed a wide freedom of choice in their individual weapons and kit. Armed with a Heckler and Koch MP5A3 sub-machine gun with folding stock, nicknamed the 'Kockler', this trooper is equipped, from top to bottom, with a hood cut from an NBC 'Noddy' suit; S6 respirator; black-dyed combat smock and trousers, personally modified with sleeve pockets, knitted cuffs and elbow reinforcement; his boots are Bundeswehr parachutist's issue. He is protected by BCME Variable Armour that can be configured to meet a variety of threat levels; pockets have been added to the front flaps. Attached to his belt at the right hip and strapped to the thigh is a commercial spring-action holster for a 9mm Hi-Power Browning pistol with 20-round magazine. A strap on the right wrist holds a spare 9mm 20-round magazine, and one on the left thigh, a leather holder for two H&K curved magazines, with a further three magazines in a

black leather pouch on the belt at the rear left h The respirator case at the rear right hip carr 'flash-bang' or stun grenades. The Type 10 Aiming Projector mounted on the 'Kockler' is high-intensity illuminating source that enables t firer to acquire, identify, dazzle and engage a tar with the 'double-tap' in total darkness or smo conditions.

G3: Argentinian Marine with Point Bla NATO/SWAT Model 30 Body Armor; Falkla Islands, 1982

The Argentinian Marine Infantry battalions whi served in the Falklands War included a hi proportion of career soldiers, and were we equipped for the campaign. This figure represent Marine wearing an example of body armour now the author's collection that once belonged to S Alfredo Vanzetti. Fitted with ceramic plates in t front and/or back pouches, it will defeat 7.62m NATO AP rounds.

H1: Israeli paratrooper with Rabintex Type III RAV Protective Vest; Lebanon, 1982

Israeli-produced Kevlar flak jackets were exte sively employed during Operation 'Peace Galilee' in the Lebanon. Designed primarily

38

fragmentation protection, the Rabintex Type III is the standard-issue body armour in the IDF.

H2: US paratrooper with Body Armor, Fragmentation Protective Vest, Ground Troops (PASGT); Grenada, 1983

Armed with an M203, a trooper of the 82nd Airborne Division near the Grenada Beach Hotel at Grand Anse during Operation 'Urgent Fury'. The Personal Armor System for Ground Troops (PASGT) embraces both the flak jacket and the 'Fritz' helmet, which are covered with 'Woodland' camouflage material.

H3: Soviet crew commander with Protective Vest; Afghanistan, 1984

This Soviet BMP commander is depicted during Operation 'Goodbye Massoud' in the Panjshir Valley. His protective vest is composed of steel alloy plates and a synthetic ballistic fibre. Since the *mujahideen* use few mortars and little artillery, these flak jackets are worn principally by vehicle crewmen, expecially in BMPs, because of the spalling inside the crew compartments when hit by machine gun fire. He is armed with a 5.45mm AKR 'Krinkof', the sub-machine gun variant of the AK-74 family; and carries on a shoulder strap an ShM respirator with an improved filter canister to protect against 'Yellow Rain' (Tricothecene toxin) and other chemical weapons used by the Soviets in Afghanistan.

In the last quarter of the 20th century more and more armies are realising the efficacy of body armour as an essential item of military equipment. With his 5.56mm FAMAS assault rifle at the ready, a French Marine paratrooper stands guard in the former residence of the French ambassador to the Lebanon, wearing a typical modern flak jacket. (French Military Attaché, London)

Acknowledgements

Many organisations, individuals and technical publications were consulted during the preparation of this book, and the author extends his gratitude to those that proved helpful. Of published references, the following were especially fruitful:

Ballistic Materials and Penetration Mechanics, Ed. R. C. Laible

Battlefield Protection of the Soldier through his Clothing/Equipment System, US Army

Helmets and Body Armor in Modern Warfare, Bashford Dean

Helmets and Body Armour Development in the 20th Century, Dr R. G. Shephard

Personnel Armor Handbook, US Navy

Police Body Armor, International Assoc. of Chiefs of Police

Wound Ballistics, US Army

The works of Martin J. Miller, Jr.

The following body armour manufacturers provided much useful material: Armourshield Ltd; BCME Ltd; Du Pont Co.; Galt Glass Laminates Ltd; Norton Co.; Point Blank; Progressive Apparel Inc.; Protective Apparel Corp. of America; Rogers Browne & Richards (London) Ltd; Second Chance Body Armor Inc.; Security Equipment Supplies Ltd.

My thanks to the following agencies: *Armor*, *Infantry* and *Soldier* Magazines, and the *USMC Gazette*; DRIC; D11 and the SB of the Metropolitan Police; HQ USMC, History & Museums Div.; Imperial War Museum; Islamic Unity for Afghanistan; Ministry of Defence (PR); National Army Museum; Office of USAF History; Royal Ulster

Constabulary; SCRDE; US Army Military History Inst.; US Naval Historical Center.

And to the following individuals, for their invaluable assistance: Marshall Carter (USMC Retd.); Mike Chappell; W. Y. Carman; Geoff

Cornish; Eric Ford; Lt.Col. George Forty (Retd. Josh Henson; David Isby; Wayne Mutza; Mart and Katie Pegler; Martin Windrow, and Stev Zaloga.

Notes sur les planches en couleur

A1 Les '*bombers*' qui tirent leur nom de la grenade à main britannique '*Mills bomb*', étaient des soldats spécialisés dans l'emploi de grenades dan des raids de tranchée. Ce soldat porte l'armure protectrice *Chemico*, pour protection contre des fragments de ses propres grenades dans les combats serrés. Son arme de corps à corps est un gourdin d'aspect médiéval fabriqué à partir d'une balle de polo cloutée de balles. **A2** La cuirasse '*Lanciers*' est portée ici par une sentinelle, exposée aux balles de tireurs isolés du fait de ses fonctions; son casque est équipé avec le troisième modèle de la visière '*système Polack*'. **A3** Le modèle tardif de '*Sappenpanzer*' porté par ce soldat d'une '*Sturmkompanie*' possèdait une barre métallique sur l'épaule droite pour la stabilisation de la crosse du fusil et des crochets pour l'équipement porté sur la poitrine. Le casque M1918 fut distribué en petites quantités vers la fin de la guerre.

B1 Ce canonnier aérien porte la veste blindée d'aviateur *M1*, le tablier blindé *M4* et le casque *M4*. **B2** Un des très rares exemples du port de vêtements blindés par les troupes britanniques durant la seconde guerre mondiale; le vêtement blindé *MRC* fut distribué aux pilotes de planeurs durant l'opération Arnhem. **B3** Ce pilote de *Superfortress* porte la vest blindée d'aviateur. *M2*, sans plaque arrière, car le siège blindé le protégeait, le blindage d'aine *M5* pour aviateurs et le casque *M5*.

C1 Ce soldat de la célèbre brigade turque envoyée en Corée est entièrement équipé d'articles américains, y compris la veste blindée *M12*. **C2** Les *US Marines* furent responsables de l'emploi de blindages de corps en Corée pour la première fois; l'armée américaine fut forcée de commander de grandes quantités du blindage *M-1951* des *Marines* dans l'attente de la livraison des modèles *M-1952* pour l'armée. **C3** Vers la fin du siège de Dien Bien Phu, environ 200 vestes blindées américaines furent parachutées à la garnison et elles furent particulièrement utilisées par des artilleurs tels que ce canonnier sénégalais du 4e Régiment d'Artillerie Coloniale.

D1 Ce *Marine* à Hue porte un blindage *M-1955*, décoré de slogans—contre les règlements, mais typique. **D2** Les commandants de tanks au Vietnam étaient en danger s'ils se montraient dans la *cupola* de la tourelle; cet homme du *11th Armoured Cavalry Regiment* porte le blindage *M69* et le casque '*CVC*', qui donnait une protection presque équivalente à celle du casque en acier *M1*, quoiqu'il soit fabriqué à partir de nylon. **D3** Blindage corporel 'variable', très lourd, porté par un soldat de la *US 9th Division* dans les conditions très pénibles des marécages de Rung Sat.

E1 Un blindage de corps en céramiques et des jambières blindées d'acier protègent ce membre de l'équipage d'un hélicoptère, alors qu'il se penche au dehors. Les illustrations plus petites montrent la partie avant d'un blindage *T65-1*, de modèle plus ancien, décorée d'une cible par forfanterie, et une arrière du blindage de port normalisé, avec un slogan typique. **E2** Un canonnier dans un bateau de patrouille de rivière, portant un blindage au titane/dérivé nylon, couvert de slogans guerriers en vietnamien; l'un d'entre eux, '*Line loi*' se traduit approximativement par 'Je suis désolé à cet égard...'

F1 Le blindage américain *M69*, muni d'un revêtement de protection britannique, est porté ici avec les jambières blindées et le casque anti-émeutes émis pour les services de sécurité civile. **F2** Ce blindage très lourd pour experts de défusage des bombes a pour fonction d'assurer, selon les vétérans 'que l'expert est enterré entier'. **F3** Le *M69* présenté ici possède le dernier modèle de revêtement de protection britannique, ainsi qu'un sac de premiers secours à l'épaule droite et des poches pour une radio émission-réception. Un blindage dissimulé est également distribué de nos jours pour port sous l'uniforme.

G1 Le blindage '*Hardcorps 3*' est porté par de nombreux services de la police américaine et il arrête les balles de plupart des petites armes, mais non des armes militaires à haute vitesse. Le blindage porté par le chien arrête une balle de 0,38. **G2** Ce cavalier *SAS* porte le blindage *BCME Variable Armour* qui peut être préparé pour arrêter divers projectiles différents selon les circonstances. **G3** Quelques exemples de ce blindage commercial de l'infanterie de la marine d'Argentine furent pris dans les îles Malouines.

H1 Le blindage *Rabintex type III Kevlar* est réglementaire dans les forces israéliennes. **H2** Le *PASGT*, système comprenant à la fois un blindage de corps et le casque *Kevlar* '*Fritz*' est maintenant introduit dans les forces américaines et il fut utilisé pour le combat pour la première fois à Grenade et au Liban. **H3** C Ce blindage soviétique, en plaques d'alliage d'acier, sert principalement aux équipages des véhicules blindés en Afghanistan; le véhicule de transport *BMP* a la réputation de se remplir de fragments mortels s'il est touché par un tir de mitrailleuse extérieur.

Farbtafeln

A1 Die '*Bombers*', die ihren Namen von der britischen Handgranate '*Mills Bor* erhielten, waren Soldaten, die für Überfälle auf Schützengräben auf Grana spezialisiert waren. Dieser Soldat trägt *Chemico*-Schutzkleidung, damit er Nahkampf vor den eigenen Granatsplittern geschützt ist. Seine Nahkampfwa ist ein mittelalterlich aussehender Schlagstock mit einem Polo-Ball u Gewehrkugeln. **A2** Der Wächter, der Schaftschützen ausgesetzt ist, trägt de '*Lanciers*'-Brustharnisch. Auf seinem Helm befindet sich die dritte Ausführung d '*visière système Polack*'. **A3** Die spätere Ausfürung des '*Sappenpanzers*', die die Soldat einer '*Sturmkompanie*' trägt, hat auf der rechten Schulter ein eisernes Band den Gewehrkolben sowie Haken, um die Ausrüstung an der Brust zu befestig Nur wenige M1918-Helme wurden gegen Kriegsende ausgegeben.

B1 Dieser Bordschütze trägt die *M1* Flieger-Panzerweste, den *M4* Panzersch und den *M4* Helm. **B2** Eines von wenigen Beispielen von Panzerausrüstung britischen Truppen im Zweiten Weltkrieg. Segelfliegerpiloten erhielten für ' Arnhem -Einsatz eine *MRC*-Panzerausrüstung. **B3** Dieser *Superfortress*-Pilot tra eine *M2* Flieger-Panzerweste ohne Rückenplatte, da ihn der gepanzerte S schützte. *M5* Flieger-Leistenschutz; *M5* Helm.

C1 Ein Soldat der berühmten Türkischen Brigade in Korea, der völlig n amerikanischer Ausrüstung versehen ist, einschliesslich der *M12* Panzerweste. Die *US Marines* trugen in Korea als erste Panzerjacken. Die amerikanische Arm musste riesige Mengen der *M-1951* Marine- Panzerausrüstung bestellen, währe sie auf die Lieferung der *M-1952* wartete. **C3** Gegen Ende der Dien Bien Ph Belagerung wurden ca. 200 amerikanische Panzerwesten mit Fallschirmen a Garnison abgeworfen, die insbesondere von den Artilleristen wie dies senegalesischen Schützen des 4. Kolonial-Artillerie- Regiments getragen wurd

D1 Dieser *Marine* bei Hue trägt eine *M-1955* Panzerausrüstung i aufgekritzelten Parolen—das ist zwar gegen die Bestimmungen, aber typisch. Panzerführer in Vietnam waren in Gefahr, wenn sie sich im Panzerturm zeigt Dieser Soldat des *11th Armored Cavalry Regiment* trägt eine *M69* Panzerausrüstu sowie einen '*CVC*'-Helm, der ihn fast genau so gut schützte, wie der Stahlhelm, obwohl er aus einer Nylonmischung gefertigt war. **D3** Eine s schwere 'Verstellbare Panzerjacke', die hier ein Soldat der *US 9. Division* in d mörderischen Rung Sat Sümpfen trägt.

E1 Diese keramische Panzerjacke und Beinschutz aus Stahl schützt die Hubschrauberbesatzungsmitglied, wenn er sich weit hinauslehnt. Die eingese zten Bilder zeigen die Vorderseite früherer *T65-1*-Panzerjacken mit aufgemalt Ziel als Herausforderung, sowie die Rückseiten der normalen Panzerausrüst mit typischen Aufschriften. **E2** Ein Schütze in einem Patrouillenboot mit ei Panzerausrüstung aus Titan-Nylonmischung mit aufgekritzelten Kriegsparo in vietnamesisch. Eine dieser Parolen, '*Line Loi*', bedeutet so viel wie 'es tut leid...'

F1 Die amerikanische *M69* Panzerausrüstung hier mit einer britisch Schutzbedeckung und mit Beinschutz sowie Strassenkampfhelm für d Sicherheitsdienst in der Stadt. **F2** Veteranen sagen über diese sehr schw Panzerausrüstung für Sprengstoffexperten, 'dass sie dafür sorgt, dass m wenigstens unzerstückelt begraben wird'. **F3** Die hier gezeigte *M69* verfügt ü die neueste britische Schutzbedeckung und hat eine Erste-Hilfe-Tasche an d rechten Schulter und Taschen für ein Zweiwegeradio. Heute gibt man au verdeckte Panzerausrüstungen aus, die unter der Uniform getrag werden.

G1 Viele amerikanische Polizisten tragen die *Hardcorps 3*-Panzerjacken, die meisten Kleingewehrkugeln abhalten, militärischen Schnellfeuergeweh allerdings nicht standhalten. Die Panzerweste für den Hund hält eine .38-Kug ab. **G2** Dieser *SAS*-Soldat befindet sich im Einsatz gegen Terroristen und trägt *BCME Variable Armour*, die man je nach den Umstände auf verschied Geschosse einstellen kann. **G3** Einige Beispiele dieser kommerziellen P zerjacken wurden auf den Falkland-Inseln von argentinischen Marineinfant ten eingenommen.

H1 Die *Rabintex Type III Kevlar*-Panzerjacken gehören bei der israelischen Arm zur Standardausrüstung. **H2** Der *PASGT*, ein System, das aus Panzerjacken u '*Fritz*' Kevlar-Helmen besteht, wird derzeitig in der amerikanischen Arm eingeführt; es wurde zum ersten mal auf Grenada und im Libanon eingesetzt. Diese sowjetische Panzerausrüstung aus Stahllegierungsplatten wird vor all der Besatzung von Panzerwagen in Afghanistan: der *BMP*-Transportwa hatte bereits den Ruf, dass er sich innen mit tödlichen Splittern füllte, sobal mit Maschinengewehren beschossen wurde.

40